Open This Book

oh good, you did.

Open This Book

The Art of Storytelling for Aspiring Thought Leaders

By Sara Lohse

Squiggles, doodles, and illustrations by Jasmine Designs

FAVORITE DAUGHTER MEDIA

First Edition

Published by Favorite Daughter Media, LLC
www.favoritedaughtermedia.com

sara@favoritedaughtermedia.com

Cover and illustrations by Jasmine Designs
www.jasminedesigns.com.au

Dedication

This book is dedicated to all the storytellers looking to find their voices and all the supporting characters in my own story who gave me permission to use my outside voice.

Foreword

Written by Joe Saul-Sehy

Stories. They've become the lifeblood of my business existence, and lucky you…you've picked up the right book to send you on a powerful journey into better storytelling.

Of course, there's a story about me, but you'll meet me later in the book, so Sara will detail how we met. At first, you wouldn't think I'm into stories. My podcast, Stacking Benjamins, is all about being better with money. I believe that if we educate more people so that we all experience financial stability (and maybe even financial success), our world is a better place. Too many people worry about their paycheck and their wallet to focus on happiness.

Yet, so many are left behind. A study by a group called Nonfiction Research found that nearly half of us report that we've cried about money. Cried. You'd think these people are living paycheck-to-paycheck or struggling with generational poverty. While that's true, they also found that people making $250,000 per year or more are also crying about their money, and only at a slightly slower rate than the paycheck-to-paycheck group.

We clearly have a problem. What's troubling is that I hear "I don't know where to turn" from people over and over. There are countless books, podcasts, YouTube channels, magazines, and so many blogs online, that finding resources and authors isn't difficult. So if there are lots of people willing to help, how come we're all still miserable with money? Why don't we know how to get help?

This book has your answer: **there aren't many storytellers.**

I'm excited about this project because Sara is about to teach you an important lesson. You and I, if we're trying to share any message, need to be good with a story. We need to know why stories are important. We need to know how great stories hit us in the gut. We need to know the situations where a story beats a pitch (or enhances it), a collection of stats (or enhances them), or a bundle of straightforward words. While a story is considered by some to be the longest way to a point, it's the shortest way to your memory, and to changing how you act.

Sara is the perfect person to tell this story, because her own story has touched people, including me. You'll read this story later, but when Sara approached me, she didn't know that the Stacking Benjamins Show receives over seventy pitches a week, from people hoping to appear on our podcast or Instagram live shows. She didn't know that most of these pitches are horrible. Sure, they were good at proving how smart the guest is, but not at all great at finding any connection. Do you want to connect more often? **Learn to tell a story.**

You'll learn from Sara that great stories imply great listening. To craft a good story you need to begin with the audience. Who are you speaking to? What are they worried about? What is the noise somewhere in the middle between the message you're communicating and their ears? You'll need to find common ground between your goal and theirs. When Sara and I sat on a bench and discussed her boss' story, it was okay. He's a great guy and later we included him on the Stacking Benjamins podcast...but later. However, Sara told her own story very, very well. Well enough that I wanted her on our show immediately.

Do you know why Sara's story connected? It was honest, raw, and about a topic only one person in the world knew about: Sara. Nobody else could tell that story. Not one.

Lucky you, she's going to teach you how to tell your story over the course of these next pages.

I think you might be picking up this book because you feel like you need a bigger platform, a wider audience, and more experience. All wrong. Sara's boss had a FAR bigger platform than Sara and her personal story landed her the spot on our show first. You have those same stories inside of you. Stop looking outside for validation and instead look at your own point of view.

I'm happy to tell you that Sara's going to lead you down that very exciting path. Embrace your own uniqueness, as she has, and you're well on your way toward more connection, more influence, and a happier existence. You have the right teacher. Now you just have to go get it.

What are you waiting for? Turn the page! She's waiting to tell you stories right around the corner.

Joe Saul-Sehy
Creator & Co-Host
Stacking Benjamins Show

Author's Note

Please don't be afraid to ruin this book. Write in the margins. Write over the text. Add your thoughts, scribbles, and doodles wherever you see fit.

If writing in a book gives you icky feelings, you can use sticky notes. But I want you to know that I give you full permission to cover my thoughts and insights with your own until the words are barely legible. Don't keep your thoughts confined to your head. Let them spill out of you like champagne at a celebration.

Just don't dog-ear the corners, you monster.

Table of Contents

Introduction

Being open and honest about who you are—whether it's in a personal setting or in the professional sphere—is not easy. Some of us have chapters of our story tarnished by trauma. Some of us have things from our past that we're ashamed of. Some of us are just struggling to find our voice.

If you're like me, maybe it's all three.

That's okay.

It took me several years to reach a point where I am somewhat comfortable in not only telling my story but allowing it to empower me. Looking back, I can trace the baby steps that led me here. By sharing those steps with you, I aim to empower you to do the same.

They say everybody has a story. I somewhat disagree.

I think everybody *is* a story. We are anthologies. We have beginnings and middles and ends. We have supporting characters and unsupportive characters. We have conflicts and plot twists and antagonists to defeat and sometimes we need a new point of view.

Our stories are ongoing sagas that shape who we are and how we're seen in our professional circles. They're full of lessons and opportunities. Your story is singularly yours, and it's never too late to steer it, to shape the narrative you desire, and to see how it can drive your career forward.

So, why do our stories matter? Because if we can harness our stories and tell them in a way that inspires connections and oozes authenticity, we can use them to build authority. When we master our stories, we can establish ourselves as thought leaders, build our personal brand, and captivate any professional audience.

Despite being intended for professional development, this book is incredibly personal. In order to teach on using stories and being authentic, I needed to drink my own Kool-Aid. This book is not written as a textbook; it's a compilation of my own personal stories—from miscalculated decisions to professional successes and everything in between—and I hold nothing back. It may feel, at points, that we've stumbled into memoir territory. I hope you'll forgive me. I promise, each story I tell has its purpose.

I include case studies and examples from different aspects of life and I also include a lot from my own—like the Maid of Honor speech I gave at my best friend's wedding. In order to learn about storytelling, I need you to be reading stories.

By sharing my stories, I hope to ignite the spark that will help you uncover yours and use it in your own journey to thought leadership.

This book is for:

- Entrepreneurs looking to humanize their brand and connect more deeply with their audience
- Professionals striving to set themselves apart in a competitive marketplace
- Creative spirits hoping to articulate their journey and leverage it in their industry
- Anyone who's ever felt they have a story within them but didn't quite know how to tell it

This book also doubles as a sort of workbook/journal. There are writing prompts and blank pages throughout, challenging you to start identifying and crafting the stories that have had the greatest impact on your life. When you get to these pages, don't hold back. Treat the book like a therapist if you need. Pop open a bottle of wine and sit in your thoughts as you ponder back in time. By opening this book you've proven you can both listen to commands (nice title, eh?) and given yourself permission to become the sole focus of your attention. At least for a little while.

This book is a call to action for anyone who has ever sensed a story bubbling within them but didn't quite know how to harness its power. Whether you're navigating the complex world of business, forging your creative path, or simply yearning to articulate your journey more authentically in your career, this book will be your guide.

I'm excited to begin this journey with you.

PART 1

Using My ~~Inside~~ Outside Voice

> *"Great stories happen to those who can tell them."*
>
> Ira Glass

Chapter 1

The Common Misconception

L et's get one thing straight right off the bat: yes, you have a story. Yes, your story matters.

I speak on podcasts and stages across the country about how we use our stories, and the first thing I hear from everyone is the same: "I don't have a story."

How could that possibly be true? You've lived a life up until this point. You've experienced *something*, haven't you?

What I think they mean to say is this: "My story isn't valuable."

We live in a world of 24-hour news cycles, social media, and a whole lot of propaganda. We've been led to believe that unless your story is dramatic, traumatic, or sensational, it doesn't deserve to be told.

The fact is, we can't all be Malala. We can't all be Anne Frank or Dr. King or the subject of a future biopic. That's okay.

In this context—and I'm generally speaking in the context of thought leadership—our stories are not meant to shock the world or inspire a nation. This is not to discredit any of the inspiring people I mentioned or didn't mention. Their stories are undeniably exceptional and should remain in history books in perpetuity.

But smaller stories matter too. The stories we share are meant to help build connections between us and those who are listening. Connections come from shared experiences.

When you hear about an entrepreneur that came from homelessness and became a billionaire, you can get inspired and awed, but unless you come from a similar background and have those shared experiences, you don't feel a connection to that person.

When you hear those little stories of people who are just doing their best and experiencing small wins here and there, you can see yourself in their shoes and feel compelled to root for them because you've been exactly where they are at some point in your journey.

Your story doesn't have to be big or earth-shattering to be impactful. That's really the point. Your story simply has to be told in a way that is honest, authentic, and shares who you are and what you've experienced.

So, how do you get to this point? How do you develop a story that accurately reflects who you are and can help you accomplish your personal and professional goals?

My goal for this book is to answer those questions and more, but I'll start with telling you my own story.

"The only real mistake is the one from which we learn nothing."

Henry Ford

Chapter 2

The Girl With
The Penis Tattoo

There is one story that started it all for me, and it was neither dramatic nor traumatic. In fact, for many years it was simply a story I would tell at a bar to fill an empty silence. That story has had a greater impact on me than I could have ever imagined. So, here it is. My villain origin story.

When I was 23 years old, I took a solo trip to Ireland, wandered into a tattoo shop, and walked out with a tattoo that looked far more like a penis than I was expecting.

That's the short version, at least. And for years, that's all I thought the story was.

So, how did that story change my life? As they say, it happened slowly and then all at once. Let's start from the beginning.

The Long Version

I graduated from Towson University in 2017 with two bachelor's degrees, one in psychology and one in mass communication. Right out of college I started in the marketing industry in the creative department of an advertising agency, writing and developing multimedia marketing campaigns and proving that even retirement communities can benefit from a well-placed pun (whether they wanted to or not).

I had coworkers I adored, clients I respected, and a boss who made me an Easter basket the first year my parents decided I was too old to be mailed one. It was a great job, but nothing is ever perfect.

I was in a rut. I was a copywriter and social media manager, and while I was learning a lot on the job, I didn't feel fulfilled. I had recently started taking antidepressants and anxiety medication and had felt a growing need to get out of Maryland and find something new.

Eric Brotman, a client of the agency I was working in, after falling in love with my writing style and talent (his words, not mine), asked me to leave the agency and join his firm as marketing manager. I said no on principle, but I wanted to be the one to tell my then-boss that the topic was broached, in case it were to come up later.

Her response became the words that I'd repeat to myself so many times in the future: "Why would he want you? You're just a copywriter."

At the same time, I had rekindled a relationship with the man I thought I would marry. I did what many young people do when they're in love: try to capture the red flags like a 10-year-old on the playground.

Why did we break up to begin with? Well, he had gotten arrested and was at this time serving a sentence in jail.

Don't worry, it gets worse.

He was in a program that allowed him to leave the jail during the day to work in the community. And, while he was outside of the jail walls, he had a phone.

We got back in contact and soon got back together. True love knows no barbed wire boundaries.

While he was working in the community to reduce his sentence, I was booking us a trip to Santorini, Greece where (in my mind) we were set to get engaged. I also signed the lease and moved into our new apartment.

Two weeks after his release, he was back behind bars.

I finally threw in the towel. I was left with a broken heart and emotional damage that would someday pay off my therapist's new car, plus a trip to Greece already paid for and the vacation days already approved.

So, I canceled Greece and put the money toward a solo trip to Ireland.

By this point in my life, I thought I had done so many brave things. I had moved to Maryland from New York for college and never looked back. I had toured around Europe and spent three months living in Florida when I was 20 just to experience something new.

I had willingly gotten into a rental car with a Bumble match I had never met and let him drive to Ohio to ride roller coasters… Okay, now that I've written that out, it may have been more stupid than brave. Please do not do this.

With all of the "brave" things I had done, I didn't think traveling to another country alone would scare me. I was wrong. I was terrified for months leading up to the trip.

The trip was a week long with stops in Galway, Cork, and Dublin. I had used a tour company to book it so that I wouldn't have to worry about getting from city to city by myself but planned to skip all the tour parts and do my own thing.

Despite being in busy cities with people all around me, this trip was the first time in my life I felt like I was truly alone. Instead of scaring me the way it had in theory, that feeling empowered me.

I spent the week doing exactly what I wanted when I wanted to. I fell in love with buskers singing on the street and, while getting lost hiking on seaside cliffs, I ended up having dinner with 30 Canadians (yes, they were as nice as people say). I made friends with locals and tourists alike, some of whom I still keep up with on social media.

After spending the weekend bar-crawling through Dublin with a group of strangers, the trip was coming to an end. On the final day, I found myself getting a tattoo of an airplane on my left arm to commemorate the experience and remind myself to always find the next adventure. You already know how that turned out.

Well, that's the story that started it all.

I came home, got the tattoo covered with an actual airplane before my parents saw it, and went back to my normal life. But my normal life suddenly didn't feel like enough.

I had been beholden to Maryland because the man I had loved said I was. My department heads had told me that I no longer seemed to be trying to impress them. They were right. I had lost the fire that made me strive to do great work because I felt like I would never be seen as more than just a copywriter. The girl who had flown across the world in search of more was suddenly settling for less.

So, I quit.

I left the job, I left Maryland, and I left behind the feeling that simply existing was the same thing as living.

I moved to Austin, Texas in July of 2019 and started a job as a marketing manager for a board game company. I thought it was the perfect start to my new life. I loved board games! Unfortunately, it wasn't. My anxiety got worse and I needed to take a Xanax after every meeting with the CEO.

I was being given goals that didn't make sense and felt like I was being set up to fail. Did I ever bring it up? Nope. Despite the bravery I had discovered, I still hadn't found my voice within a professional setting.

Within five months, I was fired. That is one thing that had never happened before. I felt like a failure, but I also couldn't ignore the feeling of relief that was creeping over me. I never wanted to be in a position where I couldn't stand up for myself.

Remember: before I moved to Texas, I had been offered the marketing manager job by Eric. We had stayed in touch and I was doing some freelance writing for him in my spare time.

A few weeks before I lost my job, he asked me to write a job description for a marketing manager. I did. He then asked me to accept the job.

The company, which celebrated its 20th anniversary in 2023, had never allowed remote work. This was 2019, pre-pandemic, so remote work was still a rarity.

He offered to buy out my lease. He offered moving expenses. But something in me knew that returning to Maryland would be a step backward.

Then I got fired. I called Eric and told him I would take the position if he allowed me to work from Texas.

I offered to take a salary lower than what I was offered in order to cover travel expenses so I could visit the office once a month to handle any projects that needed in-person attention.

I had lost my job on Friday. I accepted my new job Monday.

Accepting the job nearly doubled my previous salary and gave me the freedom to work from home with my rescue pup as my office manager. I was happier, freer, and more respected.

Most importantly, I had found my voice.

When Eric was my client, I had heard him and his team complain about the lack of financial literacy in schools. When I became an employee, I explained my plan to fix the problem. I was determined and, despite initial hesitations, was given the green light to do more than I could imagine. More on that later.

In the next months and years, the client who became my boss also became my business partner when we launched a media company and joined the fight against financial illiteracy. This is when things started to fall into place a bit faster.

In 2021, I was at a podcast conference, representing the podcast I produced and looking for opportunities to grow the show. Joe Saul-Sehy, the host of the Stacking Benjamins show, was there, too, and I was on a mission to meet him.

When I say I "stalked" him for three days, I don't want you to get the wrong idea. I'm not being dramatic for the sake of the story. I didn't simply try to talk to him if I saw him in the hall or go to his presentation hoping to catch him off stage. No, it was far worse.

I stood at a cocktail table holding my signed copy of John Lee Dumas's book in front of my face while I pretended to read but actually watched Joe from a distance and planned my next move. I may as well have held a newspaper with eyes cut out in front of my face. I am not ashamed, though I probably would be if it hadn't worked.

When I finally approached him, I actually yelled, "I've been casually stalking you for three days and if I don't get my host booked on your show I will be fired."

By some miracle (or because I'm five foot tall and highly unintimidating), he gave me his number so we could meet the next day and talk about how we could make that happen.

"I can't let you get fired," he had said. "We'll figure something out."

When we met, I gave a big pitch about Eric and how he's an expert in all things financial planning and would be a great guest on Stacking Benjamins.

Joe patiently listened to me ramble, but when I was done, he explained, "I don't need experts on my show. I need people with really cool stories."

I had no idea how to respond to that. I don't know Eric's stories, and I didn't think a response such as "I'm sure he has some!" would have been sufficient.

Do you see where this is going? Well, Joe didn't. Because the next words to come out of my mouth were not what he was expecting.

"Do you want to hear the story of when I got a tattoo of a penis while I was in Ireland?"

Believe it or not, he did want to hear that story. We sat on a bench in the middle of the conference center and I told him about the bar crawl through Dublin with the strangers I met and the tattoo artist who apparently didn't like tourists very much.

He loved the story. He loved how I told it. And that, my friends, is how I accidentally got myself booked on Stacking Benjamins (we did get Eric booked, too. And I kept my job. Don't worry).

I credit Joe with a lot when it comes to the turns my career took after that, but not just because he gave me a platform to tell my story. He's the one who found the value in it. He heard it as a life-changing experience that altered my mindset, improved my professional status, and inspired me to take more chances. He didn't view it as a silly story to tell at a bar.

He guided me through the story on his show in a way that pulled out valuable messages and impactful insights that I didn't know were hidden between the inked lines.

That was the day I realized that our little stories do have value, even if we don't see it right away.

Rewriting my own story showed me that a story doesn't have to be headline-worthy to be worth telling. I became a better storyteller, grew into my passion for thought leadership, and launched a company that changed my life.

Now I'll Try to Sound Smart to Make Up For The Embarrassing Story I Just Told

Why did I tell you a story about an embarrassing tattoo in a book that is meant to garner your respect for my professional expertise? That's a really great question I am sure my editor will also bring up. I told you that story to prove a point: every story can have value if you take the time to find it.

Is there a rule about not including obscure movie references in books? I hope not, because I am about to.

One of my favorite movies is called About Time, released in 2013 and starring Rachel McAdams, Domhnall Gleeson, and Bill Nighy. The short version of the premise is that Tim (Gleeson) inherits the ability to travel through time from his father (Nighy).

He can only travel to past moments in his own life, so he can't "kill Hitler or shag Helen of Troy," but he does have the ability to relive key moments and make changes.

His father, who we learn is dying, gives him the secret formula for happiness:

| Step One | Live every day of your normal life, just like everyone else. |

| Step Two | Go back and live each day again, almost exactly the same, but taking the time to see past the tensions and worries in the world that stop us noticing how sweet the world can be. |

In his "step twos," we get the details we didn't see the first time. We see the kindness in a barista's smile, feel the joy of a legal victory, dance to the music we had tried to ignore, and appreciate the comfort and love of his wife (McAdams).

What stayed with me from this movie (other than, well, all of it), is this quote from Tim at the end:

"And in the end I think I've learned the final lesson from my travels in time; and I've even gone one step further than my father did. The truth is I now don't travel back at all, not even for the day. I just try to live every day as if I've deliberately come back to this one day, to enjoy it as if it was the full final day of my extraordinary, ordinary life."

I want you to look at each of your days in that way. Think back to the days that felt ordinary and pull out those small moments of extraordinary. Move forward from this moment with the intention to notice them the first time.

The story I told took place in 2018, and began to have value in 2021. I am sitting here writing this in 2024. A lot has changed in the last three years.

I am now a business owner, a professional speaker, a podcast host and producer, and, by the time you're reading this, a published author.

There are so many stories I could tell if I only made it a point to remember them.

I challenge you to try. Here's a few ways:

Daily Reflections

At the end of your day, pretend you are able to timetravel and go back to the beginning. Who did you meet? Who did you speak to? What did they say to you? Did you overhear an impactful statement while walking down a sidewalk? What did you feel as you went through each phase of your daily agenda? Some of these moments might seem ordinary, but within them, there often lies a nugget of insight or an unexpected twist that's worth exploring.

Write Things Down

Carry around a small notebook and a pen and write down the moments that you want to remember later. Yes, voice memos and phone notes work, too, but there is something extra special about writing things down.

Pay Attention To Emotions

Personally, I struggle with anxiety daily and my emotions are often all over the place. But those surges of emotions that we feel—whether its joy or pain or anxiety—often indicate that something important is happening. What is it?

Talk

I have mixed feelings about conferences (my anxiety and dislike of crowds being the cause of most of the negative ones) but I go to several every year. My favorite part about conferences is how everyone is ready to talk to someone else. People share their life stories while in line for a coffee. They give the secrets they spent years learning to the stranger at the table next to them. This is the part of a conference I wish would spill over into everyday life. Talk to as many people as you can throughout a day and remember what they teach you.

Pay Attention to Details

When you pull out your notebook because something feels worth writing down, write down the little details, too. The beauty of small stories lies in the details. The warmth of your grandmother's hands, the aroma of your favorite childhood dish, the rustle of leaves during an evening walk—it's these details that breathe life into a story.

Where do we go from here?

I start by encouraging you to be an open book, and by doing that I am making a promise to be the same. I normally tell my story in a much more condensed and far less personal way, but that's not what this book is about. Now it's your turn.

The rest of this book will be filled with insights, inspiration, and more anecdotes from my life and work. I hope you will take the time that is needed to really think through what you want to say and how you want to tell your story.

If you visit this book's content guide, found at www.favoritedaughtermedia. com/book, you'll find a printable journal filled with the writing exercises I present in this book. Download it. Print it out. Use it.

Write down your stories and pick through them. Find the value. Find the lessons. Find the power that will push you to be heard.

When you're done, please reach out to me to share the story you've written. I'd love to read it.

What to Remember

Embrace the Power of Personal Stories: Those laugh-out-loud, eyebrow-raising moments in your life are the chapters of your story that inspire, teach, and connect. Never underestimate the impact of sharing a piece of your journey, no matter how silly or small it might seem.

Discover Hidden Value in Your Experiences: Every experience, no matter how small or insignificant it may seem, holds value. It's important to reflect on these experiences to uncover hidden lessons and insights that can contribute to personal and professional growth.

Transformative Power of Storytelling: The way you tell your story doesn't just change how others see it; it transforms how you see it too. A simple event, when shared with intention and reflection, can reveal layers and lessons you never realized were there, influencing both you and your audience in profound ways.

What to Do Now

Think back to a moment that seems small or insignificant on the surface—maybe it's a conversation that went sideways, a comical mix-up, or a day that just felt off.

How did this event shift your life, your choices, or your outlook? Write about this experience with a focus on the details and the emotions of the moments. What did you learn and how did it change you? Start looking for the value in your existing stories that you didn't see before.

Journal

Journal

Journal

Journal

Journal

Journal

"A goal without a plan is just a wish."

Antoine de Saint-Exupéry

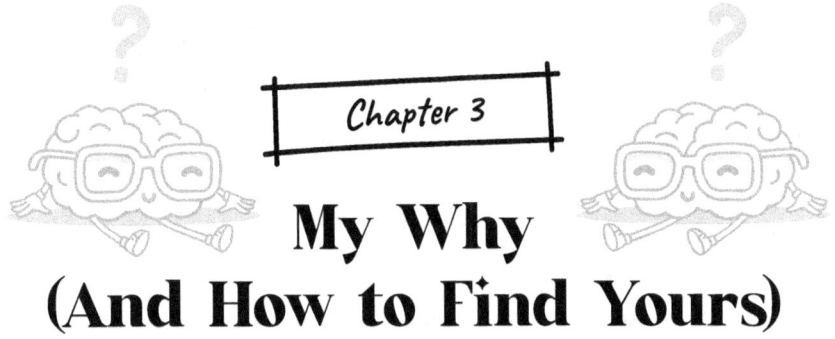

Chapter 3

My Why
(And How to Find Yours)

During my senior year of college, I took a class on public speaking and speech writing. Throughout the semester, I had to stand up in front of a classroom of at least a dozen other students and give a speech I had prepared and written on note cards.

I was fully contemplating dropping out of college each day I had to walk into that classroom. I remember the first speech I gave in that class. It only had to be two minutes. For that entire two minutes, I forgot how to inhale and nearly fell over as I walked back to my seat. Public speaking was not for me.

So, how did I grow into the role of thought leader? How did I end up in a position where a book I write may be helpful to someone else?

I wanted to make an impact.

Thought leadership isn't just about talking on a stage, hosting a podcast, or creating content because you want to be heard. Becoming a thought leader is about carving out a unique space where your ideas, expertise, and insights shine.

Becoming a thought leader begins when we recognize the limited viewpoints of the status quo and the need for change. We need to kick that status right in the quo and offer up a perspective that we know is valuable but hasn't yet been told.

My Whys

Wherever and however we decide to make a change, it always sparks from an internal driving force. I call this force our "why" (not very creative, I know).

We have different whys for different changes. We also sometimes find our whys after we've already started working on them.

Here are a few of mine:

My Why: Because finance needs to be for everyone

I never thought I'd find a passion related to finance. Not only did I have no desire to be anywhere near finance professionally, I had very little understanding of personal finance at all. I thought a 401(k) was a charity race and that is far too much running.

The only experience I had in the finance industry was an internship at Mariner Finance while I was in college. I was hired in the marketing department as a copywriting intern to help with rewriting their website and creating content for social media.

I noticed pretty quickly that there were a lot of men there, which was made more obvious when our department lunches would be held at The Tilted Kilt (an Irish-themed version of Hooters).

I was planning out content for social media and we were approaching International Women's Week. There were women at the company, so I suggested we highlight some of them in social posts with quotes or pieces of advice that could be inspiring to young girls who may want to work in finance or another male-dominated field. The response I received was, "We don't want to get political."

That was the day I learned two things:

1. To be a woman is a political statement.

2. I will never again work in finance.

Naturally, when I was offered the marketing manager position at the financial advising firm, my answer was "no." There may have also been a four-letter word in front of the no, at least in my head.

It took a lot of convincing for Eric to change my mind. He offered me $60,000 as the starting salary. I was making $45,000 at the board game company—and that was only because I lied during my interview about how much I was making at the advertising agency and said I wouldn't take a pay cut. Career advice: Lie?

I was only 24 and $60,000 seemed like a very generous salary—nearly double what I was being paid at the ad agency. Knowing I wouldn't take it, I countered at $80,000 just for fun. He accepted. I nearly cried, but still turned it down.

When I lost my job and called Eric back, I knew it would be hard to convince him to let me work remotely. I offered to go back to his original salary offer and let the difference cover the travel costs of flying me to Baltimore as needed. We negotiated more details, and eventually we had a deal.

That didn't change my feelings about the industry, though. Not only was I less-than-excited to work in a "man's industry," I had a very negative opinion of financial planning as a whole. In my mind, it was a playground for the rich, a service dedicated to helping the wealthy get more wealthy. Thankfully, the company had already thrown out the rule book on only hiring men and had more gender diversity and women in leadership than I'd seen in a lot of industries. However, they still strictly served the wealthy.

What's the saying? If you can't beat 'em, change 'em? No? Well, it is now. I had found my why.

After two years of having the firm as a client, I had heard them say repeatedly how shameful it was that personal finance isn't being taught in schools and how financial illiteracy was becoming an epidemic.

I decided that if I was going to be subjected to the horrors of the financial world, I would do it in a way that I could be proud of. My first order of business was to create an online course for middle and high school students to learn the basics of personal finance (saving money, how a credit card works, how to pay for college, and the like). I also, to the shock of the executive team, planned to offer it for free.

They were skeptical. "Free" is not generally in the vocabulary of financial service companies. They let me do it anyway.

I teamed up with the younger advisors to create the course and after a few weeks, it went live. They thought they had appeased me. They were wrong.

Next on my agenda was free monthly webinars and then more and more educational content. They agreed to all of it. Maybe financial professsionals aren't all that bad?

In 2020, we launched Brotman Media Group, a sister company fully focused on creating free or low-cost resources to help spread financial literacy. I was vice president.

I worked mostly with Eric on these projects, including publishing his book, "Don't Retire... Graduate!: Building a Path to Financial Freedom and Retirement at Any Age," which went on to win several awards. His business partners were paying attention, though. Throughout 2020, Lena Nebel, chief operating officer and, as of 2024, president, and Yanni Niebuhr, chief investment officer, worked with Eric on streamlining their processes and developing a new service offering that would remove the biggest barrier of entry to financial advice there was: asset minimums.

In 2021, BFG launched the Financial Planning for All program, effectively eliminating the $600,000 asset minimum previously required by the firm and making quality financial planning services accessible to more families and individuals across the country.

I never spoke publicly about my plans for financial literacy education. The content I created was published under the name of an advisor (they had the credentials). But I became a thought leader for the first time. My audience was simply my colleagues, rather than the public, and I was making my voice heard and ensuring that viewpoints and opinions did not go ignored. The team embraced my perspective more deeply than I ever expected, and to say I am proud of the changes they've made would be a gross understatement.

Sparking change doesn't have to be global. Changing the opinions or behaviors of just one person, one group, or one company is an accomplishment.

My Why: Because great podcasts deserve great guests

When I accepted the job at BFG Financial Advisors, I inherited the responsibility of overseeing their podcast, "Don't Retire... Graduate!" As I began taking on more roles at the firm, including my promotion to director of marketing, my responsibility regarding the podcast increased. I became the executive producer.

Now, "podcast producer" can have different definitions depending on who you ask. For me, it meant I was in charge of everything from setting the recording schedule and booking guests to writing out the show descriptions and promoting the episodes. Someone else handled editing, thankfully.

Getting more involved in the process meant learning more about the podcast industry. I attended conferences all over the country, met other creators, and learned the best practices from those who knew more than me.

One of the things I learned—mostly by watching it go wrong—was that being a great podcast guest was not an inherent skill. I listened to countless podcasts where the guests (or hosts) made me want to stop listening. When those guests were on the show I produced, I got to make the always fun and not awkward at all call to tell them that, "I'm so sorry, something went wrong with the audio file and we won't be able to release your episode."

I know, I'm a coward.

But when you see so many people do something well or poorly, you start to pick up patterns. I started to craft a formula for what makes a great podcast guest.

When I launched Favorite Daughter Media, my goal was to teach that formula to others so that they could leverage podcasts as a marketing tool while creating great content that the producer is proud to release.

My Why: Because everyone has a story but not everyone knows it

This is my why for writing this book. Not only have I been told "I don't have a story" more times than I can count, I also have been the person thinking I didn't have one.

When I learned how to reframe my silly tattoo story as a valuable self-discovery experience, it opened my eyes to the impossibly high number of stories that go untold every day simply because their teller hasn't found the reason to tell them.

My whys have grown, evolved, and multiplied over the years, but there was a never a time that I didn't have one nagging me to do more or keep going. Our whys are what drive us to make changes, so we need to identify them.

Finding Your 'Why'

I didn't write this book because I wanted to see my name on a book cover. I have photoshop, that would've been way easier. I wrote it because I am so passionate about storytelling and thought leadership that I just needed to share my ideas with someone else. Maybe someone would read it and learn something. Maybe not. If you are reading this, thank you from the bottom of my heart. Either way, I was working toward my why of empowering other thought leaders.

Finding your own why isn't always easy. It involves digging deep and getting uncomfortably honest with yourself.

Go make yourself a cup of tea, grab a soft blanket, curl up in your favorite chair (we need to be uncomfortable emotionally, not physically), and ask yourself these questions:

What Are My Core Values?

Identify the values that are most important to you. What principles guide your decisions and actions?

What Activities Energize Me?

Reflect on the tasks or activities that leave you feeling energized and fulfilled. What common thread runs through these experiences?

What Am I Passionate About?

Consider what topics or issues you feel strongly about. What could you spend hours talking about without losing interest?

What Are My Natural Talents?

Think about the skills or talents that come naturally to you. How do these influence your choices and goals?

What Positive Impact Do I Want to Make?

Envision the kind of impact you want to have on others or the world. What legacy do you want to leave behind?

When Have I Felt Most Fulfilled?

Recall moments in your life when you felt truly fulfilled. What were you doing, and why did it bring you such satisfaction?

What Problems Do I Enjoy Solving?

Identify the types of challenges or problems you enjoy tackling. What about these situations appeals to you?

Who Do I Admire and Why?

Think about people you admire or look up to. What qualities or achievements do they have that you aspire to?

What Would I Do If Money Were No Object?

Imagine having all the financial resources you need. What would you choose to do with your time?

How Do I Want to Be Remembered?

Consider your legacy. How do you want people to remember you, and what do you want to be known for?

What Are My Core Values?

_____

_____

_____

_____

_____

_____

What Activities Energize Me?

_____

_____

_____

_____

_____

What Am I Passionate About?

_____

_____

_____

_____

_____

_____

_____

What Are My Natural Talents?

What Positive Impact Do I Want to Make?

When Have I Felt Most Fulfilled?

What Problems Do I Enjoy Solving?

Who Do I Admire and Why?

What Would I Do If Money Were No Object?

How Do I Want to Be Remembered?

Transitioning from 'Why' to 'What's Next?'

Once you know your whys, you need to start looking ahead. How can you take your whys and translate them into tangible goals?

In order to begin your thought leadership journey, you need to set goals that are not just aspirational but actionable.

Let's say your driving force is empowering young entrepreneurs. Your goal as a thought leader could then be to create a mentorship program, launch a podcast addressing the challenges they face, or write a how-to guide based on your experiences. The key here is to make sure your goals are aligning with your whys so your path forward feels not just strategic, but deeply personal and fulfilling.

Setting goals as a thought leader also means setting a course that's both ambitious and realistic. You want to aim high while acknowledging the steps it'll take to get there.

Break down these larger goals into smaller, manageable stepping stones that, when combined, build a mountain of accomplishments you can look back at with pride.

Here's an example:

GOAL

Drive innovation in my industry.

Stepping Stone 1: Identify what areas of the industry are most in need of change.

Stepping Stone 2: Identify how my skills, experience, or knowledge could begin to make those changes.

Stepping Stone 3: Start creating content—blogs, webinars, podcasts, and articles that shares these ideas with others.

Does changing an industry sound easy? Of course not. That's why thought leadership is so important.

We identify what changes need to be made and start talking about them, which begins a butterfly effect. As people hear you speak, read your articles, or interact with your content, they can join you in your efforts.

Could I have changed the financial advising firm to no longer have asset minimums? No, I barely understand what that means and should never be trusted to do math. But I could start talking about why change was important, inspire others, and watch the power of many have a greater impact than one person alone.

What Are Your Goals?

SMARTen Up Your Goals

What are SMART goals? We hear about these a lot. They're goals that are Specific, Measurable, Achievable, Relevant, and Time-bound.

Break down your goals into concrete, achievable steps with clear timelines.

Specific:

I will achieve [specific objective] by focusing on [specific area of improvement or development].

Example: I will increase my podcast's listener base by focusing on enhancing content quality and guest variety.

Measurable:

I will measure my progress by [specific metric or standard].

Example: I will track the number of new subscribers and the engagement rate for each episode.

Achievable:

I will achieve this goal by [actions or strategies].

Example: I will collaborate with well-known guests and promote the podcast through social media and networking.

Relevant:

This goal will help me [how this goal contributes to broader objectives].

Example: Growing my podcast will establish me as a thought leader and expand my professional network.

Time-bound:

I will accomplish this goal by [specific date or time period].

Example: I aim to achieve a 20% increase in subscribers within the next six months.

Remember, your why and your goals can evolve. Life's a journey, not a rigid plan. As you grow, your perspectives might shift and your goals might need some tweaking. That's okay.

Revisit your goals every so often and reevaluate the steps you need to take to reach them.

Your Turn

Write out your goals and break them into clear SMART steps.

Journal

Journal

Journal

> "Choose to show up for yourself.
> Then, actually do."
>
> Ash Ambirge

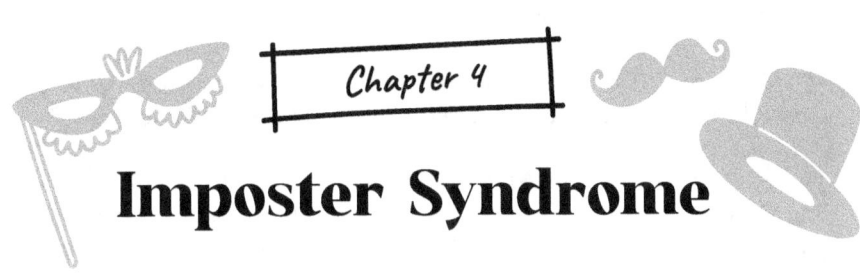

Imposter Syndrome

The president of a Fortune 500 company stands on stage in front of thousands of employees to talk about the company's new strategic plan.

A graduate student stands in front of a panel of professors to defend her dissertation on climate change.

An actor is called to the stage to accept his first Academy Award.

All three of them are thinking, "I don't belong up here."

As I write this book to encourage you to speak up and share your stories and ideas with the world, I need to acknowledge the most common reason I have heard people give for not having started already: imposter syndrome.

Understanding Imposter Syndrome

Imposter syndrome, or imposter phenomenon, is the recurring feeling that you aren't enough, don't deserve your success, or don't belong in the position you hold. Whether it's your first day at a new job or a week from your retirement date, you will experience it. It's part of the human condition.

Dr. Susan Albers-Bowling of the Cleveland Clinic explains imposter syndrome as "the feeling that everyone else knows exactly what they're doing, but you feel lost. You have this fear that the people around you are going to figure out that you don't know what you're talking about and expose you as a fraud.[1]"

A lot of people who experience imposter syndrome credit their successes and achievements more to luck than to their own merit. This is something I find interesting.

Think back to something you worked incredibly hard for. Did you ever tell someone about it, only for them to respond with "wow, you're so lucky?"

I started noticing this trend when I built my house. I would tell someone I am building a house and they'd say, "wow, a house? You're so lucky."

This idea that good things come from luck rather than work is basically ingrained in the psyche of our society. After the umpteenth time I was told I was lucky, I had to start setting them straight.

"No, I actually worked very hard for this."

Either they'd look at me like I'm rude, realize their error, or both. That's what we need to start doing. We need to start setting ourselves straight because usually it's our own mind telling us we're lucky.

Watch for those thought patterns next time you accomplish something, and set yourself straight.

You are not lucky.

You worked for this.

You earned it.

You deserve it.

How to Fight Imposter Syndrome

"Why would someone listen to me?"

"Who am I to write a book?"

"My opinion isn't important."

I hear these objections daily when I talk to others about thought leadership. Usually, it's the imposter syndrome talking.

I spoke at Outlier Podcast Festival in May of 2023. My topic was on the different ways you could use your podcast to grow your business. I had prepared talking points, had index cards, and stayed up late memorizing everything I wanted to say. When I stood up in front of the audience, I felt like an expert on my topic, but I didn't feel like an authority. I wasn't proving my knowledge by reading pre-set words off of index cards.

I felt like an imposter.

Then my presentation was interrupted by a hand in the air. I was asked a question and the answer wasn't written on my cards. I had to pull the answer from my experience and I delivered it thoughtfully and honestly. Her question was answered and she got the information she needed.

I continued my presentation with noticeably greater confidence because I had proven to myself that, believe it or not, I actually knew what I was talking about.

Then it got more interesting. The next question wasn't about the content of the presentation. A woman stood and asked why people would need to hear what she has to say. She was describing her own experience with imposter syndrome.

I stood in front of that room with my blonde hair in pigtail braids, a floral denim overall dress, and Chuck Taylors. I basically looked like I had gotten lost coming back from recess and accidentally ended up at the front of the room with a microphone in my hand.

"Do you think I, this overgrown toddler standing before you, truly believe that everyone in this room needs to hear what I have to say?"

Of course, I didn't think that. But I did know that I had information on this topic that others did not have and I was offering it up to whomever felt like attending this session.

Sometimes, however, it's other people talking.

When I attended a public speaking workshop in February of 2024 I was, by far, the youngest in the room. I noticed. Everyone noticed. Still, I was there to speak on a panel and wore my event badge that said "Speaker" under my name with my head held relatively high.

The first session had the imposter syndrome starting off strong.

We were seated at round tables of about five or six people and were instructed to go around the table and give our elevator pitch for why someone should want to work with us. We would then get feedback from the rest of the table.

I gave my pitch and braced myself for the feedback (I've never been good at handling criticism, even when it's constructive). One woman, we'll call her Lisa because that is her name and I'm petty, offered her feedback first.

"I am so much older than you and have way more life experience. What do you really expect to teach me at your age?"

Side note: Don't be Lisa.

Her comment came like a punch to the gut. She said aloud the words that the voices in my head were already saying.

As rude as it was, it also gave me the opportunity to respond not only to her, but to those internal voices.

"You have more years of life experience than me, that's true. But you do not have *my* experience. What I have to teach I learned while finding success doing things that you have never done. It doesn't matter how old I am. Everyone has something to teach."

Did that feel good to say? Honestly, I think I blacked out from the anxiety but my friends at the table filled me in later and it sounded very satisfying hearing it back.

It wasn't about answering her, though. It was about convincing myself that I do have something to teach.

With your lifetime's-worth of experiences, no matter how many years that may include, there will always be something that you know more about, understand better, or have a different viewpoint on than other people. Every person who has written a book or given a TED Talk or presented at a conference knew a little bit more than their audience. What makes you and I any different?

And so, my first and best piece of advice for how you can fight imposter syndrome is to do exactly what I did: acknowledge it. Don't be afraid to feel those feelings of not being worthy of the position you're in. But when you feel them, address them. Remind yourself that it is the imposter syndrome thinking those negative thoughts and you have just as much of a right to share your knowledge as everyone else.

By simply recognizing that what we're feeling is imposter syndrome, we can stop it in its tracks. Bullies lose interest when you don't let them see they're impacting you. Imposter syndrome is nothing more than an internalized bully.

Once you've acknowledged your feelings, here are a few more things you can do to fight imposter syndrome:

Remind yourself of how you got to where you are.

Make a list of your achievements and the skills you used to accomplish them. Use that inventory of awesomeness to remind your brain that you deserve everything you've worked for.

Avoid comparing yourself to others.

Forget about the Joneses and what everyone else is doing. We have a tendency to compare ourselves and where we are to others despite our paths being incredibly different. The comparisons are never fair, as we compare ourselves to those with more or different experience. You can't look at yourself in your current chapter of life and compare yourself to someone in a completely different book. Let your own path stand alone and cheer on those whose paths intersect with yours.

Remember that success is not a limited resource.

The idea that intangible things can be unlimited is widely accepted in other contexts. Nobody (outside of Matilda's parents and other ungodly fictional villains) welcomes in their second child only to realize that they have enough love in their hearts for just one baby. Love has no limits.

Well, neither does success. Someone else finding success does not remove the possibility of you also being successful. We are far too civilized to still be in the dog-eat-dog mindset. Let others have their wins and celebrate with them. Let them celebrate with you when it's your turn. Don't let someone else's success make you feel unsuccessful.

Celebrate your successes.

Whether it's in a social media post, with a party, or by stopping for your favorite treat on the way home, allow yourself to celebrate each win and success you experience. Make a big deal out of what you do well to balance out the negativity when things don't go as perfectly.

Treat yourself the way you treat others.

This is my preferred golden rule. We grow up being told to treat others the way we'd like to be treated, but it's rare we offer ourselves the same kindness and grace that we give out.

Don't be so hard on yourself when you stumble or have a set back. In those moments when you're feeling like an imposter, think about what you'd say to a friend who was struggling in the same way.

Welcome mistakes as opportunities for growth.

When you make a mistake or have a small failure, learn from it, reframe it as a lesson, and use it to propel yourself forward.

What to Remember

Prevalence of Imposter Syndrome: Imposter syndrome hits all of us, regardless of age, success level, or title. It's the feelings of inadequacy and the fear of being exposed as a fraud, despite a history of success.

Recognition and Acknowledgment: The first step in overcoming imposter syndrome is acknowledging it. Understanding the cause of these feelings and reminding yourself of your achievements can stop them in their tracks.

Overcoming Imposter Syndrome: Reminding yourself of personal achievements, avoiding unfair comparisons, celebrating successes, and embracing mistakes as growth opportunities are a few ways to battle it.

What to Do Now

Let's celebrate some successes.

Write down the skills and accomplishments you're proud of. List the wins you've had recently. Think about the people you most often compare yourself to and write down a few lessons you can learn from them, rather than reasons for judging yourself.

Journal

Journal

Journal

Journal

PART 2

Storytelling

"There isn't a stronger connection between people than storytelling."

Jimmy Neil Smith

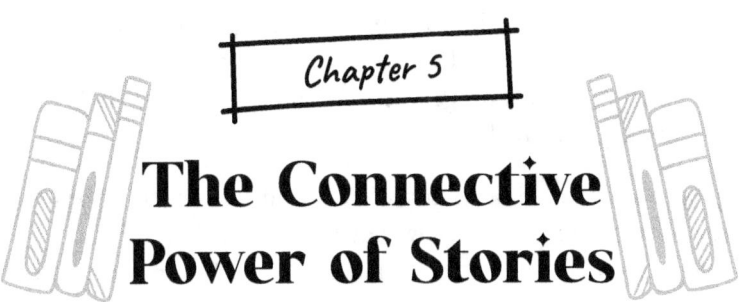

Chapter 5

The Connective Power of Stories

If we're trying to be seen as experts and authorities, why would we focus on stories rather than on information?

Simple: information isn't compelling.

In late 2023, I had a conversation with a gentleman named Brian Gorman, a professional coach who is passionate about communication and stories. In our conversation, he shared two stories with me.

He had a client who was responsible for delivering the safety briefings to employees of a manufacturing firm. If you've ever flown on an airplane, you're probably as guilty as I am of turning up the volume of your music when the safety lecture starts. It's the same thing every time and we all doubt we'll ever really need to know what to do in the event of an emergency water landing.

The employees at this manufacturing company felt the same way. He couldn't get them to pay attention to his briefing, despite the importance of the information.

"I know how important this information is. I grew up without my grandfather because he was killed in a workplace accident."

The power and emotion behind those two simple sentences give them more impact than an entire lecture. He began incorporating that personal story into the briefing and it changed the way the information was received.

The second story Brian shared was about a series of conferences focused on organizational change that he attended in the 90s. He was able to tell me about two keynote speakers. One was a guide in a reserve in South Africa who talked about the resilience of wild animals, tying it to the theme of resilience in the workplace. The second was a dentist who shared how and why he, as a dentist, is an agent of change, tying the story back to the theme of organizational change.

Each year, I attend at least six conferences and see countless speakers give presentations. There are very few that I can remember by the time I get back home from the event. It has been nearly 30 years since Brian saw those two men give their keynote presentations and he can still remember them because they told stories that he was able to connect with.

"It's the story that sticks with me. Not just the words, but the message."

The Neuroscience of Storytelling

Anecdotal evidence of why we should tell stories is great, but did you know there's actually scientific evidence of it, too?

I am not a scientist. I want to make that very clear. However, I have studied the work of scientists who have studied the brain, how it reacts when we hear and tell stories, and the general conclusion is this: our brains are wired for storytelling.

This is Your Brain on Stories

Through studying brain imaging, neuroscientists discovered a phenomenon called "neural coupling."

When we listen to a story, our brain activity mirrors that of the storyteller, particularly in regions responsible for language comprehension and processing[2].

This discovery reveals why stories resonate so deeply with us. When we listen to a story, in addition to processing words, we're experiencing the events in a synchronized, neurological harmony. This explains why stories can evoke empathy, stir emotions, and leave a lasting impression.

You've experienced this. Think about the last time you watched a scary movie.

The main character has made the age-old mistake of running toward the creepy noise instead of away to safety (despite how many times you yelled from your couch for her to turn around). The music picks up in that suspenseful way, and what happens? Your heart starts to beat quickly and you're overcome by that awful feeling of dread and anxiety. This isn't because you're experiencing the danger, but because your brain is mirroring the emotions of the person in the story.

As a storyteller, this insight is invaluable. It means that the way a story is told—its rhythm, its imagery, its emotional arcs—can directly influence the listener's brain activity.

I mentioned in the first chapter that stories come from shared experiences. If you tell your story well and you create a strong neural coupling, it's almost like you're tricking the listener's brain into thinking this is something you experienced together.

Tips for Sparking Neural Coupling

Vivid Imagery

Use descriptive language to paint a picture in the listener's mind, engaging more senses and letting their brain become immersed in the setting.

Emotional Connection

Craft stories with emotional depth to resonate deeply with your audience's experiences and feelings. Lean into how you felt during the experience you're talking about and portray that in the way you tell it.

Clarity and Pace

Tell your story clearly and maintain a steady pace to keep your listeners' brains in sync with yours.

The implications of this study extend far beyond a scientific understanding of storytelling. It underscores the power of a well-told story to not just convey information but ignite a deep, empathetic connection between people. It reveals that in every act of storytelling, there is a potential for profound human connection.

If you'd like to read the full study, you can find a link to it on this book's content guide found at www.favoritedaughtermedia.com/book.

It's Purely Chemical

You're probably familiar with oxytocin: the hormone/neurotransmitter most often associated with love. It's part of the neurotransmitter trio of happy hormones (oxytocin, serotonin, and dopamine) that make us act like foolish little school children when we're around someone we're attracted to.

Oxytocin is also an important chemical when it comes to storytelling.

Research by neuroeconomist Paul J. Zak has shown that a compelling story can stimulate the release of oxytocin, leading to increased empathy and emotional connection between the storyteller and the audience[3].

In his study, Zak found that good stories increase oxytocin production, enhancing the listener's sense of empathy and making them more receptive and generous. This biochemical change shows that a good story can have a profound impact, even affecting our decision making.

What makes a story so good that it creates a chemical reaction? There are three key elements you want to think about:

Tension

A good story needs a good conflict. Tension creates a sense of urgency, a need to know, a compulsion to stay tuned. Aim to build up the curiosity so that your listeners can't help but follow along. It's what turns passive listeners into active participants who are emotionally invested in the outcome.

Relatability

Relatability is the bridge that connects your story to the hearts of your audience. It's found in the universal truths, the shared laughs over life's absurdities, the collective sighs at its complexities.

When a story is relatable, it whispers (or sometimes shouts), "You're not alone." It's seeing a piece of your reflection in the characters, their struggles or wins, that makes the story stick long after the telling is done.

Relatability is about finding the common ground where your experiences resonate with others, making your story not just heard, but felt and remembered.

Narrative Arc

Narrative arc is the backbone of your story, giving it structure, direction, and flow. It's the journey from Once Upon a Time to them all living happily ever after, mapped out with intention.

A well-crafted narrative arc takes your audience from introduction to conflict, through rising action, climax, and resolution, in a way that feels both inevitable and surprising. It's the promise of a journey worth taking, where each twist and turn, each rise and fall, feels like a step closer to a destination that's both satisfying and transformative.

The narrative arc ensures that your story isn't just a series of events, but a journey with purpose, direction, and meaning.

A story rich in tension keeps the audience guessing, relatability brings them into the fold, and a compelling narrative arc guides them through to the end, leaving them changed, in big or small ways, by the journey you've shared.

If you'd like to read Zak's full article, you can find a link to it on this book's content guide found at www.favoritedaughtermedia.com/book.

Tips for Getting a Chemical Reaction

Focus on Emotional Resonance

Craft stories that evoke emotions, making them memorable and impactful.

Understand Your Audience

Tailor your stories to resonate with your audience's experiences and interests.

Practice Empathy

Put yourself in your audience's shoes to create stories that truly connect with their values and aspirations.

Storytelling is more than an art; it's a tool of influence rooted in our biology.

By understanding and harnessing the neurochemical impact of storytelling, we are able to create stories that captivate the audience, fostering empathy and trust, bridging gaps, and strengthening bonds between you and your listeners.

Thank You for Coming to My TED Talk

TED Talks have set the gold standard for public speaking. In 1984, the first TED conference laid the foundation for a platform that would become synonymous with influential and inspiring communication.

The way that TED Talks are structured, delivered, and shared has changed the way we communicate in profound ways, underscoring the importance of storytelling in the way we communicate.

Here's what we can learn from TED and apply to our own speaking:

Brevity and Precision

One of TED's most distinctive features is its time constraint: all talks must be under 18 minutes. This enforced brevity is a masterclass in precision—trimming the fat to reveal the meat of the message. You're driven to make your point with the elegance of a poet and the sharpness of a scientist, proving that sometimes, less really is more.

Emotional Resonance and Vulnerability

When Brene Brown stood up and spoke about vulnerability, she made herself the prime example, connecting with every person in the room and those watching on a screen. TED speakers know that to truly touch someone, you must reach out with your whole self, flaws and all. It's this raw honesty that transforms a talk from a monologue into a conversation and from a presentation into an experience.

Visual Storytelling

TED Talks are presented without presentation slides or visual aids, allowing for full attention to be on the speaker. While it lessens the distractions, it also leaves it up to the speakers to use vivid imagery in their storytelling to keep the audience engaged.

Celebrating Diversity

TED's magic lies not just in the stories told but in who tells them. It's a kaleidoscope of voices, experiences, and perspectives, reminding us that wisdom isn't held solely by any single culture, gender, or background.

Don't Just Inform, Inspire

TED teaches us that the best communication doesn't just leave the audience with something to think about—it leaves them with something to do about it. Greta Thunberg's passionate speeches on climate change exemplify this, combining education with a powerful call to action.

TED has elevated storytelling from a simple art to a pivotal tool of communication, demonstrating that the right story, told the right way, can indeed change the world. It's about packing a punch with a few well-chosen words, connecting through our shared humanity, and embracing the vast spectrum of human experience.

If you want to be great at something, you study those who are already great. Go watch a few TED Talks and pay attention to the stories they tell *and* how they tell them.

Stories and Authenticity

Using storytelling as tool goes back to a word I will use several times in this book: authenticity.

Authenticity is the quality of being genuine, true to oneself, and free from pretense. It's not about being infallible or having all the answers; it's about acknowledging your imperfections while remaining committed to your values and beliefs.

Authenticity can mean different things to different people. Because I spent years in the financial services industry, trying to shave off my square corners to fit in their round holes, I connect authenticity with self-expression.

The first time I spoke at a conference, I was asked if I planned to cover my tattoos (the answer was no). When I experimented with semi-permanent pink hair dye, I only escaped disciplinary action because my position wasn't client-facing and I worked remotely. If I were in the office, it would've been a different story. My emails featured words like "pertaining to" and "regards" and invitations to "circle back." I was doing my best to fit the mold until I decided it was a losing battle.

I left the financial industry because I didn't feel like I was able to be authentic, but I've kept my accreditation as a financial counselor because I am still passionate about helping spread financial literacy. In 2023, I was invited to speak at the Association for Financial Counselor and Planner Education®'s (AFCPE®) annual conference about how podcasting can be used to grow a financial services practice. This is the organization through which I earned my accreditation, so while I technically did belong, I was one of very few attendees or speakers who did not actually work in finance.

For months leading up to the event I went back and forth on how I should show up at this conference. Do I dust off the blazer in the back of my closet? Wear the heels with the pointed toes that make my feet bleed? Do I change my presentation to the corporate blues instead of my typical pinks?

It took me until I arrived to decide. I sat in the airport with my slides pulled up, contemplating finding someone who held a briefcase and wore a tie to ask for their feedback on the color of my presentation. I remember wanting to ask, "Would you take me seriously if you saw these slides?"

I had packed the clothes I would feel like myself in, but I also packed the professional dresses and shoes that I swore I'd never wear again. I put on the dress. I put on the shoes. I looked in the mirror and I just didn't recognize myself.

20 minutes later, I was back in my Chuck Taylor All Stars, jeans (no holes, though. I did compromise), and a brown faux leather jacket I had just bought at Marshalls that week. I looked like me.

I hadn't even remembered that part of my presentation discussed authenticity. When that slide came up, I came clean.

"I wasn't sure how to show up today. I almost wore the costume of the financial professional. But if I'm going to stand up here and tell you to be authentic, then I need to be as well. I live my life in jeans and sneakers, not blazers and slacks. But I'm up here because I have something I can teach, and I hope you'll still want to learn from me."

The presentation went well, I answered several questions from the audience, and continued to mingle and network for the rest of the event. When I got home, I saw a meeting was booked on my calendar. I hadn't met the woman who scheduled it, but she had attended my session. All she wanted was to thank me for my presentation because she had never seen someone show up so authentically and seeing me be myself, despite the fear of judgement, was the breath of fresh air she needed at that event.

Being authentic is vital and should be at the forefront of everything you do.

Why?

It builds trust.

People are more likely to trust someone who shows
vulnerability, admits to their mistakes, and shares
both their successes and their struggles. Simply put,
people trust those who are honest, and authenticity
is essentially honesty in its physical form.

Building trust can be difficult. But each time you show
up authentically, it's like you're slowly moving the pieces of a puzzle to
reveal the real you.

Of course, there is also that one kid who just peels the colored stickers
off the Rubik's Cube and sticks them back on like he "solved" it. But the
stickers never quite sit the same way again, and anyone looking closely can
tell that that something isn't right.

Authenticity requires reaching a level of vulnerability that is not always
easy, especially when it's in the public eye. But when you are honest about
who you are and showcase the peaks alongside the valleys, you give others
a reason to trust you.

It's a way of saying, "Hey, I've been where you are. I've stumbled and even
face-planted, but I've learned."

This candidness resonates with people. If you can trust someone to be
honest about their failures, you're more likely to trust their advice on
achieving success.

It makes you unique.

Your authentic self is your unique selling proposition.
It's that special sauce, the thing that differentiates you
from those around you.

Remember, everyone has their story, their experiences,
their perspectives. Nobody else has walked in your
shoes. While two people might share knowledge on the
same topic, it's their individual experiences and authentic
expressions that set them apart.

76

It helps you connect.

At our core, we as humans are social creatures. We long for connections, stories, and shared experiences. And while expertise and knowledge can certainly draw an audience, it's emotional resonance that turns an audience into a community.

When you share authentic stories as a thought leader, you're sharing facts and insights and, more importantly, you're sharing a piece of yourself. Whether it's the story of the time you had an epiphany while struggling with a major project or the lessons you learned from a mentor who changed the course of your career, these stories create bridges.

They tell your audience, "I get you. I've been there."

By sharing in this way, you're inviting others to share their stories. This two-way street deepens the bond and fosters a sense of community.

Thought leadership is about creating conversations and fostering connections.

How to Share Stories and Stay Authentic

Be True to Your Voice

Imitating someone else's style or parroting popular opinions might get you some initial attention, but it's a poor strategy for long-term credibility. Your voice is your signature; make sure it's consistent across all platforms and types of communication.

You may have noticed that this book is not written in the polished, perfect-grammarly way of most books in the business section. No, that's not some ploy to fit in with today's youth (I'm only 28, guys. I'm still hip). I write this way because it is my voice. To not do so would be inauthentic.

Share Both Ups and Downs

While it's tempting to present an image of constant success, that's rarely the reality for anyone. Sharing the challenges you've faced, the mistakes you've made, and how you've overcome them adds depth to your message and makes you more relatable.

The first story I told you was pretty embarrassing. It revealed my subpar decision making, poor taste in men, and complete inability to conduct myself professionally at a conference. But hopefully, it made me come across as a real person who made typical choices for someone in their 20s.

Our 20s were the years we all experienced heartbreak. We all went through the breakups we thought would truly break us. We got the tattoos we now hide and scars we wish would fade, stumbled through new responsibilities and let some people down, and lost jobs and friends and braincells while we tried to find ourselves.

I told you my story because, despite the missteps and misdirections, I learned and grew from all of it. But I also learned how to tell it.

Don't be afraid to share your blooper reel alongside the highlights. We've all made mistakes and we can't erase them, but if we change the way we tell them and start focusing on the value, our ups and downs can guide and impact other people.

Acknowledge Your Evolution

Your views and opinions will change over time, and that's okay. Acknowledge your evolution and update your stories to reflect that growth. Authenticity doesn't mean being static; it means being honest about your journey, including the shifts and turns.

If you change your mind or learn something that shifts your perspective, share the change and talk about why. Your learning moment can become someone else's.

I had a terrible headshot when I worked in finance. Driver's license-level bad. It was stiff and grey and barely recognizable, even to myself. Now, my headshots feature pink dresses, bright backgrounds, and a smile that's genuine. The evolution was so severe, I had to acknowledge it.

(You can see both photos in this book's content guide found at www. favoritedaughtermedia.com/book.)

The first of these pictures was taken in January 2020. The second in January 2024. What's the difference between the two?

The first photo is of a girl just starting in the finance industry, with no idea who she was or what she was capable of. She showed up the way she thought she was expected to: in business clothes with a professional smile and a firm handshake. She held her tongue and conducted herself in a manner fitting the industry (the best she could, at least).

The second photo is a different girl. She shows up exactly as she is: messy, in bright colors, with a smile that reaches her eyes. She speaks her mind, laughs at herself, and refuses to be anyone but herself.

I am proud to be both of these girls. The first one got me to where I am. She met mentors who guided her through tough times and formed relationships that would last. She learned how to find her voice and how to use it. She built the girl in the second photo.

The second photo is the girl I looked up to when I was a kid struggling to find myself. She is unapologetic about who she is, even if she isn't always sure of exactly what that means. She has learned how to be authentic and how to leave the room that makes her feel like she needs to be the first girl.

No matter what industry you're in or what your role is, always remember to show up as yourself. If who you are isn't accepted in the room you find yourself in or at the table you're sitting at, it's time to find another room with another table.

Be the person the younger you needed.

SHARE ON SOCIALS

Pitfalls to Avoid

Overexposure

Being authentic doesn't mean you have to divulge every detail of your personal life. There's a fine line between authenticity and overexposure; cross it, and you risk diluting your message and expertise.

When it comes to sharing, imagine you're curating an exhibit of your journey, not starring in a 24/7 reality show. Choose the moments that genuinely matter—those instances that spark a thought, strike a chord, or shift a perspective.

The goal isn't likes and follows, it's about meaningful connections and sharing stories that invite conversation and reflection, not just consumption.

Forced Vulnerability

Authenticity should come naturally. While genuine vulnerability can forge powerful connections, there's an obvious difference between organic openness and forced exposure.

Ever been told to "act natural" and then you suddenly forget how to stand like a person? That's because being natural is not an act. Sharing should come from the heart, not from a playbook, and trust me, people can tell the difference.

Instead of thinking about how you can come off as relatable or digging for tear-jerking moments that really didn't need any tears, just be yourself and tell the stories you want to tell, not the ones you think will have the biggest emotional response.

Inconsistency

When I say to avoid inconsistency, what I'm really saying is, again, just be yourself.

Consistently show up as your true self. If I showed up to the finance conference in a pantsuit when I usually walk on stage in jeans, those who pay attention and want to get to know me would notice the difference. You want your audience to feel like they know who you are, not needing to guess which version is the real you.

Thought leadership isn't about putting on a show. It's about showing up—flaws, missteps, victories, and all. Just ditch the script and speak from experience. Genuine moments of vulnerability and consistent, true-to-you messages aren't just appreciated; they're magnetic. They draw people in, turning audiences into communities.

What to Remember

Authenticity Builds Trust: Authentic storytelling, where you share both your successes and struggles, significantly builds trust with your audience. By showing vulnerability and admitting to mistakes, you create a genuine connection, breaking down the facade of perfection.

Personal Evolution is Key: Acknowledge and share your journey of growth and evolution. Change in perspectives and learning from experiences makes your storytelling dynamic and relatable. Authenticity involves being open about your journey, including the changes in your views and opinions.

Neuroscience Backs Storytelling: Storytelling is an art form, and rooted in our biology. Understanding the neurochemical impact of storytelling—such as the release of oxytocin and neural coupling—highlights the power of a well-told story to create empathy, forge connections, and influence thoughts and behaviors.

What to Do Now

Reflect on a significant change or evolution in your perspective or approach in your professional life.

Write a story that encapsulates this journey, focusing on the key moment and experiences that prompted this change. How did this shift impact your decisions, actions, or beliefs?

Make sure to include the emotions, challenges, and insights gained. Reflect on how this evolution has shaped your current perspective and approach as a thought leader.

Journal

Journal

Journal

> "There is no greater agony than bearing an untold story inside you."
>
> *Maya Angelou*

Chapter 6

You Are Now an Open Book

We all have a library of stories stored up inside of us. How do we determine which stories we tell, when to tell them, and how?

Let's talk about it.

The Types of Stories We Tell

There are different types of stories that accomplish different goals. Some are meant to connect on an emotional level. Some are meant to teach a concept in a relatable way. Some are meant to just lighten the mood in a tense setting.

Here are six key story types that you can use as a thought leader:

The Origin Story

Or, for some, the villain origin story.

This is exactly what it sounds like. How did you get to where you are? What hurdles did you have to overcome? Telling your origin story shows yourself as being relatable and approachable.

An origin story can be the story of how you got to this place in your career—your journey from your first job to current position, launching your company, or your experiences since graduating from college—or the story of how you got to this place in life—maybe you're a child of immigrants, a first-generation college graduate, or had to navigate school with a learning disability.

Telling this type of story has several benefits and uses:

Establishing Credibility

The origin story is the introduction to you as it relates to your topic. You establish credibility in the same way that showing your work on a math test does. Lay out the steps you've taken to come to the conclusion you're speaking on, proving that you have authority on your topic and aren't cheating off the kid next to you.

Winning Over New Audiences

When engaging with a new audience or trying to establish your own, sharing your origin story creates a bond by allowing people to understand your background and the values that drive you.

During Times of Change or Challenge

In moments where there might be skepticism or resistance, recalling your roots reminds people of where you came from and how you got here. It can be comforting to know that you're still that person building a dream from your garage, and you still have all the lessons you learned as the dream slowly became a reality.

Inspiring and Motivating Others

When you're speaking to a group you want to inspire, like with a commencement address at a graduation, sharing your origin story allows your listeners to learn from your mistakes and understand that hurdles aren't meant to stop your growth, they only make you find an alternate route.

Reinforcing Brand Identity or Values

When reinforcing the identity or core values of your brand, an origin story brings us back to heart of your "why." It's not just about where you're going; it's about where you've been and the core values that drive every decision you make.

Connecting on a Personal Level

When you find yourself in those closer, more personal settings, sharing your story isn't just small talk—it's a way to establish deep, genuine connections. It's the difference between a handshake and a heartfelt hug.

Take Oprah Winfrey, for example. Not many of us can relate to a woman with a net worth of nearly three billion dollars. It's not her wealth that's drawn us in—it's her story.

Oprah didn't start with much. Far from it, really. Born into poverty, facing abuse, and even homeless at 14, her early years were marked by intense struggles and situations that far more people can relate to than her current status.

Hearing how Oprah moved from those hardships to where she is now strikes a chord with anyone who's faced their own battles. It's her journey through adversity that inspires hope and the belief that it's possible to overcome seemingly insurmountable challenges. By sharing these raw, real parts of her life, Oprah bridges a gap, making her feel accessible and relatable despite her immense success.

Her origin story doesn't just add a layer of depth to the empathy and understanding she shows on screen; it roots it in authenticity. We don't just see a media mogul. We see someone who's genuine in her every action, from the interviews she conducts to the causes she stands behind. This authenticity is what has truly captured America's heart, making Oprah not just admired but deeply beloved.

The Milestone Stories

Our milestone stories are our highlight reels. They show off our biggest wins, game-changing moments, and those turns in the road that took us in an entirely new direction.

These stories typically highlight the big breaks, breakthroughs, or "a-ha!" moments—the times when everything clicked into place and we were propelled forward into something new.

They're the stories we lean into when we want to showcase our growth, toast to our triumphs, and map out how we got from there to here. Imagine standing on a stage, holding that award, and sharing not just the win, but the grind it took to get there—the hurdles leapt, the lessons etched into our playbook, and the moments of sheer determination that define our journey.

Milestone stories are a good fit when:

Celebrating Achievements

When you achieve something noteworthy, sharing a milestone story is a great way to celebrate this success. It could be a new product launch, reaching a significant number of subscribers or clients, or receiving an award. Pop the champagne and let others take part in your big moment.

Reflecting on Growth and Evolution

Year-end reviews, company anniversaries, or just a reflective Tuesday— these are perfect times to look back and talk about the leaps and bounds by which you've grown.

Motivating and Inspiring Your Team or Audience

When the going gets tough, reminding your team or audience about past glories can spark that "We've got this" spirit, pushing everyone to lay it all on the line.

Building Trust and Credibility

In situations where it's important to establish credibility, like investor meetings and client pitches, a well-placed milestone story can be your proof of performance, showcasing your knack for turning visions into victories.

Teaching and Mentorship

Using milestone stories help illustrate the power of perseverance, strategic thinking, and the courage to chase your biggest goals.

Reinforcing Vision and Goals

To remind everyone (including yourself) of the bigger picture and why you're all in, milestone stories act as benchmarks of success, underlining that the path you're on is leading somewhere pretty spectacular.

One of the most famous examples of this must be from the Apple iPhone launch event. Steve Jobs, co-founder of Apple, announced the revolutionary product that combined three devices into one—an iPod, a mobile phone, and a computer.

Instead of simply introducing the iPhone, Jobs shared the story of the iPhone's development and launch, which is now often used to exemplify innovation, visionary leadership, and strategic risk-taking. It's a powerful narrative about how a single product can change an industry and elevate a company to new heights. This milestone story continues to inspire entrepreneurs and leaders in various fields to pursue transformative innovation.

Insight Stories

Insight stories are your opportunity to bring your expertise to life. It's pulling back the curtain to reveal how the magic really happens. This isn't about bragging or showing off your wall of awards; it's about letting people in on what went on behind the scenes—the brainstorms in the shower, the "what if" moments that hit you at 3 a.m., and the journey from embarrassing first attempts to well-deserved victories.

These are your "light switched on" stories, the chapters where you connect the dots in ways no one else has. Maybe it was spotting a trend in the noise of data that everyone else missed, or applying a left-field solution to a problem that's been a thorn in the side of your industry for ages.

Don't just skip to the end and unveil the final product. Walk us through the maze with you. It's about sharing the gears turning in your head, the strategies you drafted, and the roadblocks you climbed over. Put it all together so we can see the journey from start to finish.

Use these stories for:

Presentations and Workshops

Insight stories can be used to make content you're teaching more relatable and illustrate how theoretical concepts are able to be applied in situations that your attendees have found themselves in.

In Sales Pitches or Client Meetings

Insight stories are a powerful tool in convincing potential clients of your expertise. Sharing how you've solved similar problems in the past builds trust and demonstrates competence far more than a salespitch ever will.

On Social Media and Blog Posts

Social media is great for sharing insight stories to establish your thought leadership. Regularly sharing small anecdotes or case studies helps in building a following that looks to you as an expert.

During Interviews or Media Appearances

When you're being interviewed, whether it's for a podcast, a news outlet, or on a panel, sharing insight stories positions you as a seasoned professional who has been there and done that.

When Networking

When you're at a networking event, swap your elevator pitch for a relevant insight story. With so many people being introduced in a short time, you'll stand out as someone they want to know (and remember).

The magic of a successful insight story lies both in what you did, and how and why you did it.

It's about showcasing your unique perspective and approach, making it clear why you should be listened to with clear evidence rather than unsupported claims.

Do you know how the Post-It Note was invented? It's actually a great example for this type of story.

Spencer Silver, a researcher at 3M, accidentally invented the sticky note when trying to create a more powerful adhesive for the aerospace. Instead of solving the problem he set out for, he created a solution that didn't yet have a problem.

Years later, his colleague, Art Fry, found the problem the Post-It Note solved when he needed a bookmark to remain in place during choir practice.

The idea of a repositionable, easily-removed note paper was met with skepticism, and it took 3M more than a decade to actually launch Silver and Fry's accidental invention that would soon become the company's most successful product.

Why is this story relevant?

It nails the essence of insight storytelling. It's about celebrating those random moments when a simple observation sparks a revolution. It's proof that big wins often come from recognizing the value in what might initially seem like a miss. Sharing a story like this not only illustrates your expertise but cements your status as an innovator who sees possibilities where others see dead ends.

That's the power of a good insight story—it doesn't just say you're an expert; it shows you are, in the most compelling way possible.

Tales of the Underdog

People love to root for an underdog. We all love a good comeback story. Underdog stories are not just stories of struggle, but of the grit, guts, and guile it takes to claw your way to the top. When you share your underdog story, you connect with your audience on a very personal level, inspiring them with your journey of facing adversity and emerging stronger.

These stories can be anything—from personal challenges that made you wonder if rock bottom may have a basement, professional failures that seemed career-ending, to taking on Goliath-sized challenges armed with nothing but a butter knife and a lot of determination. The gold is in the grind: the walls you hit, the times you fell, and most importantly, how you dusted off and tried again.

This is your time to be realer than real and more vulnerable than may feel comfortable. Share the nights you wrestled with doubt, the missteps that taught you lessons textbooks couldn't, and that moment of breakthrough when the light at the end of the tunnel turned out to be a new day, not a train about to run you over.

This honesty doesn't just make your story compelling; it weaves a bond with your audience and leaves them rooting for you.

Underdog stories are great for:

Motivational Speaking

When addressing an audience that needs inspiration, particularly those facing their own challenges, an underdog story has the power to spark someone else's comeback.

Team Building Activities

Sharing your own underdog story with your team inspires a culture of resilience and determination. It motivates team members to persevere through challenges and see obstacles as opportunities to work better together.

Podcast Interviews

People often turn to podcasts for inspirational stories when they need a pick-me-up. Sharing an underdog story can give them the motivation they need to keep going, while making yourself a memorable and impactful guest.

Mentoring or Coaching

In one-on-one sessions and small group settings, your underdog story provides a powerful example for mentees and protégés who may be facing their own struggles.

Social Media and Personal Branding

People want to interact with people, not brands. Sharing your underdog story and opening up on social media helps humanize your brand, bringing you followers who want to support your journey.

Autobiographical Content

Whether writing a book, a blog, or creating a podcast, including your underdog story provides depth and context to your message, making your other achievements even more impressive.

Underdog stories encapsulate the human spirit and the fight, fire, and faith that drives us during the darkest times.

This type of storytelling is a powerful tool for a thought leader, as it demonstrates resilience and determination and inspires others to believe in their own potential to overcome challenges and succeed against the odds.

We find ourselves in the stories of Michael Oher's leap from uncertainty to NFL fame, Elle Woods's iconic rise to success at Harvard ("What? Like it's hard?"), and countless others who've turned their trials into triumphs. We cheer not just for their wins, but for the winding roads that took them there—because in every underdog, we see a bit of ourselves, our struggles, and our dreams.

We follow their journeys and hope for their successes because we see the bumpy road that they had to travel and recognize our own journeys on a similar path.

A Day in the Life

What's it like to walk in the shoes of someone you admire, your favorite speaker or author that is presented with poise and polish? If it's all keynote stages and spotlight moments, would it feel real?

'A Day in the Life' stories peel back the curtain of the everyday grind—the routines, the hiccups, and those quiet (and rare) moments of clarity. These stories are your chance to bring people along on your daily journey, from the first sip of morning coffee to the last click of the keyboard at night.

It's in the little things, like how you tackle that mountain of emails with a system that's part strategy, part sorcery, or the rituals that keep your creative juices flowing even when the well feels dry. And it's about those times when the day throws you a curveball, revealing how you pivot, adapt, and keep moving forward.

Use these stories for:

Social Media Engagement

These stories are perfect for social media, where people seek authentic glimpses into the lives of those they admire. Regular posts or stories about your day help build a deeper connection with your audience.

Blogs or Newsletters

Adding 'A Day in the Life' stories in your written content offers your readers actionable insights based on the reality of your daily life, helping them understand what makes you thrive .

Personal Branding

When building your personal brand, these stories differentiate you, highlighting your distinct way of navigating both work and life.

Mentorship and Coaching Sessions

Sharing the raw cut of your daily life provides mentees with a textured understanding of the challenges and triumphs on the path to success, grounding abstract advice in lived experience.

Spotlight Speeches and Interviews

Whether you're on stage or in an interview chair, sharing a bit of your daily reality can demystify success and make your insights more accessible.

Team Meetings and Culture Building

Inside your organization, these stories can humanize leadership, encourage transparency, and build a culture of authenticity and mutual respect.

'Get Ready With Me' videos and day-in-the-life vlogs are running rampant on social media because we're drawn to the genuine and the unfiltered. They give us the opportunity to connect over the shared experiences of everyday life, making the person behind the persona feel like a friend.

Remember, the goal of these stories is to show up real and raw, in all of your messy glory. Build trust and connections while letting people see that the path to success is paved with more than just the highlight moments— it's the discipline, the daily decisions, and the dedication to your craft that truly count.

What's Your Why?

Your "why" is the driving force behind everything you do, so 'What's Your Why' stories are the heartbeat of your personal and professional persona.

These stories are the pulse of your daily life—the reasons that get you out of bed every morning and keep moving despite seemingly endless challenges.

When you share your why, you open up about what matters most to you. This vulnerability creates authenticity and helps others relate to you on a human level.

We use why stories for:

Personal Branding and Marketing

In building your personal brand, sharing your 'why' differentiates you, making your message compelling and relatable.

Leadership and Team Building

As a leader, when you share the driving force behind your vision, you're not just instructing; you're inspiring. It's about bringing your team along on a mission that matters, igniting a shared passion that turns visions into victories.

Fundraising and Pitching

For pitches and proposals, your why is your secret weapon. It transforms a simple ask into a compelling cause, engaging potential backers not just with the promise of profit, but with the addition of purpose.

Public Speaking and Keynote Addresses

On stages and platforms, weaving in your why turns a speech from a monologue into a dialogue with the hearts and minds of your audience, leaving imprints that linger long after the applause fades.

Networking and Relationship Building

In networking and relationship-building, sharing your why isn't just about swapping business cards; it's about connecting on a level where true collaborations and friendships can blossom.

Mentoring and Coaching

For mentors and coaches, sharing your 'why' helps mentees understand your approach and philosophy, making your guidance more meaningful and personalized.

Remember, your why is what sets you apart, fuels your passion, and drives your success. It's the story behind your accomplishments and the lens through which you view challenges and opportunities. By sharing this, you become relatable and provide a source of inspiration and encouragement for others to explore and articulate their own whys.

I told you my why stories earlier because I wanted you to understand the motivation behind everything that led to me writing this book. I wanted to help you get to know me, my passions, and the driving forces behind what I do each day so that you could understand me a little better—and to encourage you to identify them for yourself.

Case Studies & Testimonials

Case studies and testimonials are stories that bring your work to life. They are the before and after photos of your professional journey, showing transformations and successes and illustrating how your knowledge, strategies, or products have positively impacted individuals, businesses, and communities.

This isn't sharing a result, but sharing the steps that led to it. Boosts in revenue, leaps in efficiency, or surges in customer happiness are important details, but the hurdles faced, the creative solutions, and the ideas you brought to the table are the plot points that make a good case study a great story.

But the magic? It's in the journey. Shine a spotlight on the teamwork, the brainstorming under pressure, and the innovative pivots that led to success. This narrative depth does more than showcase your skills; it reveals your character, your approach to problem-solving, and your commitment to adapting and overcoming.

Use these stories:

In Marketing Materials

These stories are magnetic for marketing. They draw potential clients in with the promise of similar success stories, making the abstract tangibly aspirational.

During Sales Pitches or Client Meetings

Woven into a sales pitch, they're your proof of concept, showing potential clients not just what you do, but how well you do it.

On Your Website and Social Media

These stories amplify your digital footprint, turning visitors into followers, and followers into fans.

In Educational Content and Workshops

When teaching or conducting workshops, using case studies illustrate how theoretical concepts are applied in real-life situations.

In Public Speaking and Conferences

Case studies make your talks more engaging and credible. They provide tangible examples to back up your assertions and theories.

In Publications and Articles

Added into articles or white papers, they bolster your insights, lending authority and evidence to your expertise.

As with everything else, authenticity is the cornerstone of compelling case studies and testimonials.

Remember, the key to effective case studies and testimonials is authenticity. Choose stories that genuinely reflect your work and impact, ensuring that the outcomes you highlight are as real as they are remarkable. This authenticity not only underscores your credibility but also weaves a thread of trust with your audience, demonstrating the tangible value and transformation your work brings to the table.

If I wanted to explain to a business owner how important it is to understand their target audience, I could give facts and figures that make empirical sense. But there's no emotion behind the numbers to add impact. Instead, I could share a case study:

Case Study: The Stanley Brand

The Stanley cup brand (the Quencher Tumbler one, not the hockey trophy) has been around since 1913. For most of its 100+ year tenure, the company marketed predominately to workmen because the innovative, vacuum-sealed drinkware design was able to keep water cold while sitting outside on a worksite all day. The tumblers' ability to stay cold led to its position as a necessary product during workdays, on road trips, and during outdoor adventures.

Stanley's audience avatars were a 30-year-career veteran police officer and a retired Army soldier. And that audience served them well for a century.

When the women behind a popular, female-focused blog The Buy Guide posted about the 40 oz. Quencher Tumbler being the best insulated cup on the market, the product gained new popularity. Interest in the product soared and the blog creators partnered with Stanley and bought 10,000 cups wholesale, which proceeded to sell out completely in 4 days.

The women at The Buy Guide sat down with the Stanley team to help them understand how and why their product was resonating with a new audience and how they could alter their messaging to take full advantage of the new attention.

Stanley started rolling out new colors and designs to appeal to women, turning the Quencher into a collectible item by partnering with brands like Starbucks and offering limited-edition product drops.

In 2023, the company's 110th year in business, Stanley saw a 275% year-over-year increase in Quencher sales.

When you know your audience and understand what they want, you can give it to them.

Transparent recounts are the "open-book moments;" the stories that lay it all on the line—your stumbles, your head-scratchers, your "what was I thinking?" moments. Because we usually only focus on the successes, opening up about the slips and trips is not just brave; it's revolutionary.

While the other story types show the challenges as a way to emphasize the win at the end, these stories don't have to have a happy ending. They're our blooper reel. They're our "I can't believe I'm telling you this story" stories when we share the lessons that we had to learn the hard way.

We want to share our wins. We want to share our success. But we also have to acknowledge that some failures aren't springboards into future successes. They are just failures that make us start back from the top.

These stories humanize you. They're about authenticity over perfection, process over outcome. They tell the world, "Hey, I've been there too. I've messed up, I've doubted, and I've learned. And if I can get through it, so can you."

These stories can be used in:

Mentorship Opportunities

When you're face-to-face with someone looking up to you for guidance, you have the opportunity to show the not-so-golden moments from your journey. It's about passing on the wisdom that sometimes the path to growth is paved with a few faceplants.

Autobiographical Content

If you're putting pen to paper (or fingers to keys) to tell your story, weaving in those "I can't believe I did that" moments alongside the wins gives your story depth, texture, and relatability.

Social Media and Blogging

These platforms are ideal for sharing personal, candid stories. Readers crave authenticity, and showing them the grit behind the glamour can turn a simple post into a lifeline.

Speaking Engagements

Want to stand out among the other conference speakers? Instead of just another success story, share mess-ups and miscalculations. It doesn't just capture the audience; it captivates them, reminding them that mistakes happen at every level of success.

Podcasts and Interviews

During an interview, dropping in a few transparent recounts makes you more interesting and memorable. It shows listeners that it's okay to not always have the answers or the perfect plan.

Networking Events

Sometimes, the most profound connections are made over shared stories of misadventures and missteps. It's about breaking the ice by breaking the facade of perfection, inviting a genuine exchange of experiences.

Remember, transparent recounts don't always wrap up with a neat bow on top. They're the raw, unedited cuts of our life—the scenes we might wish to delete but choose to share, understanding their value lies not in the success they show, but in the humanity they reveal. By sharing these moments, we don't just tell others it's okay to fall; we show them it's possible to rise again, wiser and more resilient.

Remember when I told you I got a tattoo of a penis? Yup. That's the example here.

～～～～ Continuous Learning ～～～～

Continuous learning stories are your way of expressing your dedication to self-improvement and intellectual growth. When you attend a conference, read a book, or listen to an insightful podcast, talk about it.

Share the lightbulb moments, the shifts in perspective, and how what you learned can be applied in your life or career. By sharing these experiences, you illustrate how you actively seek out new knowledge, challenge your own perspectives, and stay at the forefront of your field.

Use these stories for:

Social Media and Blogging

Share the a-ha moments with your audience and invite them to read the book or listen to the podcast to open up doors for discussion.

Team Meetings and Corporate Training

Sharing your learning experiences with your team, and encouraging them to do the same, sparks a culture of curiosity and continued growth that will only help your company grow.

Networking Events and Conferences

Discussing interesting ideas you recently gained from books or seminars is a great conversation starter that can also provide valuable insights to those you share it with.

Mentoring Sessions

Pass on the knowledge you gained by sharing your continuous learning journey. Your mentee will learn something new and may gain practical ideas for their own development.

Keynote Speeches and Public Speaking

Incorporating new and up-to-date information into your speeches makes your content relatable and dynamic, providing fresh perspectives and insights.

Client Meetings and Pitches

Demonstrating that you are always staying updated instills confidence in clients that you are well-informed and ahead of the curve in your field.

The goal of sharing continuous learning stories is to demonstrate that growth is not a destination but a life-long journey.

As a thought leader, you want to be showing that you are evolving, value knowledge, and are always looking to improve. Plus, while you're learning new information, you're also seeing how other industry leaders are showing up in these spaces.

On my company blog, I'll share recounts of conferences I attended, interviews I did, and other instances where I learned something new so that I can both show off my new knowledge and share it with others. Recently, I was given a new point of view on one of my most often told stories (yes, of course it's about the stupid tattoo). Here's what I wrote about it:

Emotional Courage

A few weeks ago, Adam Baruh invited me on his podcast, Beyond the Microphone, to talk about the Branded podcast and how I serve clients through Favorite Daughter Media.

The conversation took an unexpected turn, however, when he brought up the term "emotional courage."

This isn't a term I'd ever heard before this conversation, but it's now one of my favorite concepts.

What exactly is emotional courage? In his book, Leading with Emotional Courage, Peter Bregman defines emotional courage as the courage to feel. I'll admit I got this definition from his book's landing page; I have not read it (though it's on my list to read).

Emotional courage is about facing our fears, doubts, and vulnerabilities head-on. Whether it's making a major life decision, navigating through personal or professional hardships, or simply embracing our true selves, emotional courage allows us to step into our power and take ownership of our lives.

On the episode, I talked about my trip to Ireland and how it became the catalyst of the change that I didn't know I needed. Facing my fears and exploring the world on my own made me more brave and self-reliant than I had been and set the gears in motion to create the life I now live.

But through podcasting, I learned how important it is to talk about those experiences. Sharing our stories and vulnerabilities can inspire and uplift those who are navigating similar struggles, fostering connections and empathy within our communities.

The beautiful thing about emotional courage is that it's not about being fearless–it's about acknowledging our fears and choosing to move forward despite them. It's about embracing authenticity, vulnerability, and empathy in a world that often encourages us to hide behind facades.

Podcasting has been an outlet for me to explore my own emotional courage in a public setting and even helped me find my voice and confidence as a storyteller. It's a medium that encourages raw, unfiltered conversations, creating a safe space for both hosts and guests to share their truths.

So, I encourage you to embrace your emotional courage, lean into your vulnerabilities, and share your stories with the world. You never know who might be inspired or touched by your words.

SHARE ON SOCIALS

This blog helped me put into words what I had learned, draw attention to my knowledge on storytelling, retell parts of my story from a different perspective, and highlight my insatiable curiosity that helps me serve my clients.

What to Remember

Variety of Story Types: Thought leadership thrives on diversity—in the stories we tell as much as in the ideas we share. Origin stories, milestones, insights, underdog tales, 'A Day in the Life' moments, 'What's Your Why' revelations, case studies, and transparent recounts—each carries its unique purpose. They're tools in your belt, ready to build rapport, establish credibility, or light a fire of inspiration and education in your audience.

Strategic Story Selection: Choosing the appropriate story type for your context—be it a keynote, a tweet, a networking event, or a mentoring session—is key to connecting deeply with your audience. It's about matching the story to the moment, ensuring your message doesn't just land but resonates.

Authenticity and Relatability: Authenticity is found in the raw, unvarnished truth of personal experience. Sharing the real deal—your challenges, your eureka moments, and your growth journey—does more than build trust; it invites others to reflect on their paths, fostering a community of authentic exploration and mutual growth.

What to Do Now

Think about each type of story discussed in this chapter and pick out a story from your own life that fits. Share how it shaped your values, beliefs, or career. Describe the hurdles, the epiphanies, and the nuances of each journey and others can learn from them. This exercise isn't just about reminiscing; it's about forging connections through the authentic sharing of your lived experience.

Journal

Journal

Journal

> *"I'm obsessed with giving the audience something they don't see coming."*
>
> Jordan Peele

Chapter 7

Choosing Our Stories

We know that we need to tell stories. We all have a lifetime of stories we can tell. Now, how do we choose which one we should tell?

This isn't as simple as "I'll just pick the ones that relate to my topic."

My topic is thought leadership.

My story is about a penis tattoo.

There are two basic methods I use to find the perfect story:

Retrospective

This is the "looking backward" method. Start with where you are now, and then think about the key moments in your life that led there.

This is sort of the Maid of Honor method. The "where you are now" is a wedding for my best friend and her new husband. As Maid of Honor, my job is to recount the key events, from a best friend's point of view, that led to these two getting married. I'm going to stand up in front of everyone she loves and tell each and every embarrassing story, drunken mistake, almost/maybe, and questionable choice that eventually ended in "I do."

And so, I did:

I've learned that in your life, if you're lucky, you find one friend that you can't live without.

I don't want to sound conceited when I say that I'm that friend for Kelli, but if you think about it, exactly two weeks after she was born someone was obviously worried that she needed a best friend and I was born. That cannot be a coincidence.

Of course it wasn't until we were in 7th grade that the universe brought us together. At a party where everyone was asleep in my basement, Kelli and I were in the kitchen with a can of whipped cream, falling over each other, in tears from a joke that I'm sure neither of us will remember. But I do remember that was the night I found my best friend.

The next few years were filled with more laughs, more dumb jokes, a few questionable boyfriends, silly fights, strange nicknames, and a year of letting her cheat off me in AP bio (which was fine because I was cheating, too). Kelli was always there for me, and I, for her.

Whether it meant driving to her house with ice cream after a breakup, staying up late to talk about our tragic teenage lives, or almost giving her mother an aneurism at 15 when she realized we'd gotten drunk right in front of her without her noticing and

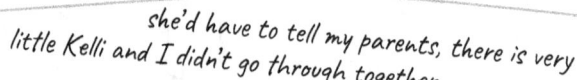

she'd have to tell my parents, there is very little Kelli and I didn't go through together.

When senior year came, we realized how hard it would be. Not academically, at that point neither of us cared about our grades. But it was the year we realized we'd be leaving each other. Rushing to get out of our small town, we both chose schools that would lead us away from each other, me to Maryland and Kelli to Arizona.

Though in my defense, I stayed within driving distance so who's really the bad guy here?

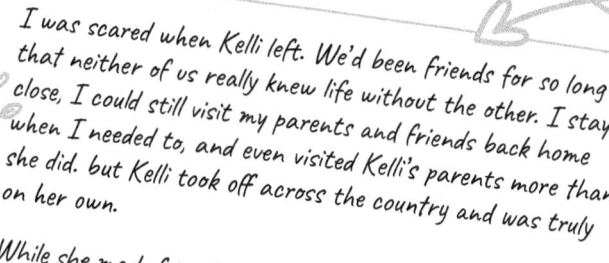

I was scared when Kelli left. We'd been friends for so long that neither of us really knew life without the other. I stayed close, I could still visit my parents and friends back home when I needed to, and even visited Kelli's parents more than she did. but Kelli took off across the country and was truly on her own.

While she made friends and had fun freshman year, I didn't stop worrying about her being lonely. Until she met Kyle.

I remember when she first told me about him. They were really good friends, she thought he was cute and maybe a little dorky. But she was worried about ruining the friendship (the classic teen drama plotline). But soon enough she was off in her new life with her new boyfriend.

I didn't know Kyle. I met him months into their relationship and still haven't spent much time with him. But for as long as they have been together, I have been so grateful for him.

Kyle, thank you for loving my best friend. Thank you for being her shoulder to cry on, her confidant, and everything I would've been for her if I was there. Thank you for protecting her, for taking care of her, and for treating her better than I've ever seen someone treat her.

To Kathy and Bob, thank you for raising a strong, independent, kind woman who will do anything for her friends or even for strangers. Thank you for taking me in as your second and possibly favorite daughter. No offense, Kelli. But I did visit them more.

To Marybeth, thank you for raising the man of her dreams, and the only person I would confidently hand her off to.

And to Kelli, thank you for loving me for half my life. Thank you for not judging me when I make mistakes, for always answering your phone when I'm crying, for being really easy to lie to when I'm flying to Arizona to surprise you, and for being the friend that I cannot live without.

For this method, ask yourself these questions:

- *What is the key message that you want someone to take away from your story?*
- *What lessons did you learn while getting to where you are?*
- *What mistakes did you make?*
- *What do you wish you would have known sooner?*

By describing the circumstances around each of your answers, you craft the story.

Prospective

This is the method for when you have a story you really want to tell. You think of the story, and then you find the ways it connects to your message.

This is the tattoo method.

I wanted to share my tattoo story that day with Joe to delay what I thought was an inevitable "no." With his help, I found the nuggets of wisdom that turned an embarrassing anecdote into a semi-inspiring story of self discovery.

For this method, ask yourself these questions:

- *Is there a story you want to tell?*
- *Why do you want to tell it?*
- *How did the experience shape you?*
- *What did you learn from it?*
- *What would you go back and tell yourself?*
- *Why should others know about it?*

The answers to these questions are your message. Write them out on the following journal pages.

Journal

How To Tell a Compelling Story

How you tell a story is just as important as what the story is. Telling a story in a way that is compelling is an art form.

For a story to be compelling, it needs to meet these criteria:

1. *It's Unexpected*
2. *It's Emotional*
3. *It's Relatable*
4. *It Has the Right Amount of Detail*

It's Unexpected

If a book is too predictable, it's boring and ends up in your did-not-finish pile, right? Your story, too, needs to be unpredictable.

You want the listener to be enticed and excited to continue listening. You want them to cling to your every word because they don't want to miss the twist in the plotline.

Now, there are several ways to craft a story to be unexpected. I have two favorites:

The Lead-In
This is the typical method of storytelling. You start at the beginning and slowly lead into a surprise ending. When well-crafted, the details that lead the reader or listener through the story should hold their attention to the end.

The Upfront
This is storytelling almost in reverse. You start with the big twist and then go on to tell the story that leads to the ending you've already revealed. It's the "I bet you're wondering how I got here" method.

As someone with intense ADHD, I love this method. I'm the person who is always trying to beat you to the end of your own story. I'm too busy trying to figure out what comes next to actually follow along with the plot of the story. Mystery novels are my enemy.

The upfront method basically spoils the ending by revealing the hook, but that hook is so unexpected that the audience really is wondering how you got there. This is a very effective way to grab attention and keep the listener engaged in real time, rather than trying to jump ahead and guess what's going to happen next.

This is another point where I often lose someone to their own self-doubt.

"My story isn't dramatic. How can it be unpredictable?"

It's all about the way you tell it.

Was my story about the tattoo all that dramatic? No. It was silly until we really dove into it.

But the first time I told it that day at a professional conference when Joe Saul-Sehy said he wanted a cool story, a story about a penis-shaped tattoo was the last thing he expected to hear. I told the punchline up front and he demanded to hear the details that got me there.

It's Emotional

The way we capture and keep attention with a story is by playing to the emotions of our audience. We portray emotion both through the story itself and through the voice in which we tell it.

You want your voice to illustrate the emotion of the story. Telling a sad story in an excited voice is confusing, telling a funny story in a monotone will take the punch out of the punchline.

Including personal details that convey the emotions you felt during the experience of the story will help listeners connect and care about the outcome. But it also means being open and vulnerable which can be scary.

It was easy for me to tell a silly story about an unfortunate tattoo, but the only value that story had was giving you a laugh at my expense.

However, once I opened up about the emotional challenges I was facing—feeling lost in my career, losing the apparent "love of my life"—you were able to see the impact that the experience had, relate through your own memories of heartache, and, perhaps, gain some courage to make a daring choice.

It's Relatable

The best way to ensure your story will be relatable is to make it personal. People care about other people and want to hear about what they go through.

The tattoo story is the example I use, not because of the story itself, but because of the personal growth it led to years later when Joe helped me restructure the way I tell it.

It is a story that nearly anyone can relate to because it's a personal experience about traveling, fear, love, and regret. We can all relate to at least one of those words.

It Has the Right Amount of Detail

Your story needs to resonate with your audience by making them active participants. Feed them details that make them feel like they can be a part of your story.

Paint a picture of the setting. Describe the emotions with precision. Let them in so that they can take something away.

But don't overdo it.

My mother (and yours, too, probably) is the reigning queen of offering too much detail. The CEO of "this meeting could have been an email."

Before I hear the very funny story that she heard from her friend at lunch, I must first know what everyone at the table ordered, what I have in common with the waitress who served them, how quickly the food came, whether or not a seagull succeeded in stealing any French fries off the table next to her, and the point of the story she tried to tell me days earlier but forgot until this very moment.

Give the details that add to the story and omit those that don't. This can be a learning experience as you read the room and see the reactions of your listeners. Keep the details that have them rapt.

What to Remember

Story Selection is an Art: There are two methods for choosing stories to share: Retrospective and Prospective. The Retrospective method is like taking a stroll down memory lane, picking out moments that have led you to where you are today. The Prospective method starts with a specific story and spins it into a message that hits home. Both ways need you to dive deep, reflecting on how each experience has molded you and your message.

Crafting a Story That Sticks: If you want your story to be the one that nobody forgets, it has to have that unexpected twist, the kind of emotional depth that gives goosebumps, and enough relatability that your audience sees a bit of themselves in it. Whether you're dropping the hook right at the beginning or leading your audience down a path to a reveal, the key is to keep them engaged with just the right blend of drama and authenticity.

The Devil (and Angel) is in the Details: Getting into the nitty-gritty makes your story come alive, but you have to strike a balance. Too much and you're rambling; too little and you're floating in the vague. The trick is to paint the picture just clear enough that your audience is right there with you, but not so much that they get lost in the weeds.

What to Do Now

Choose an experience from your life that you think is relatively mundane or ordinary and turn it into a good story.

Identify the unexpected, dig into the emotions, relate to the masses, and choose the right details to make it compelling.

Journal

Journal

Journal

PART 3

Thought Leadership

> *"Innovation distinguishes between a leader and a follower."*
>
> Steve Jobs

Understanding
Thought Leadership

If I'm going to focus on how to become a thought leader, I should probably talk about what that means.

A thought leader, in its most basic sense, is someone who is seen as an authority on a topic by expressing a deep understanding and a new perspective on the subject matter. Thought leaders drive conversations, shape opinions, and spark discussions within their industry or niche.

In today's age, a thought leader is, essentially, a content creator. That doesn't mean they're posting dance videos on TikTok (though they may be). It means they're creating some form of content meant to share their thoughts.

Content can come in the form of a podcast, social media content, educational webinars, blogs, articles, speeches, presentations, music, film— nearly everything we do that others experience can be considered content.

It becomes thought leadership content when it is created to express your authority and expertise.

That being said, I'd also like to talk about what a thought leader is not.

Thought Leader vs. Influencer

We live in an age of Influencer Culture. When I think of influencers, I think of Instagram models and TikTok makeup artists. These are people who we see wearing an accessory or using a product and we want to buy it because, wow, they're cool.

I think of the Marlboro Man and how he was so pretty, he got an entire generation addicted to cigarettes. Fun fact: He dated my mom in the 70s. Not-so-fun fact: He later died of respiratory failure.

Influencers sell products and impact behavior because of their aesthetic. They cause you to stop scrolling.

Thought leaders make you stop and listen.

Now, if a thought leader is already an authority, why do stories matter? Why not simply rely on knowledge?

Two reasons.

1. We're no longer in an information desert. The invention of the internet and smartphones means that at any given moment, we can Google a topic and be presented with more information about it than we will ever actually read. So, when joining the global conversation about the topic, we cannot rely on the facts we know to help our voice be heard over the noise. It is the new perspective presented through a lens of personal experience that cannot be found on a Wiki page.

2. As you've probably experienced, the invention of the internet also gave way to a growth of parasites commonly referred to as "Internet Trolls." People will argue with anything you say and try to find holes or any excuse to call you an idiot. However, as much as they cut down or try to disprove your facts, they cannot argue with your stories. Nobody can say, "No, this person did not experience that."

Well, they can say it but nobody will listen.

Let's jump back to Outlier and that question from the audience. Was I ever under the impression that everyone in the room needed to hear what I had to say?

I was not. But I was pretty sure they wanted to. I was asked to speak at this event because I knew more than the average person about my topic. The event had several sessions happening at once, and attendees had a choice of which speaker they wanted to see at that time. My room was packed.

There's a strange misconception when it comes to putting our thoughts and ideas into the universe. It's like people think that because we're talking, we expect the *entire world* to stop and listen.

The entire world was not my audience that day. The group of attendees at this particular event that had more interest in my topic than the others in that time slot was my audience.

We are thought leaders, not thought dictators. Those who have interest in the topics we speak on will find our message. Don't let imposter syndrome tell you that nobody wants to listen to you. The entire world may not need or want to hear your story, but someone will.

What It Really Means

In 2023, I was interviewed by Authority Magazine about effective communication and asked what I would list as the characteristics of an effective communicator. They are also the traits of an effective thought leader. Here was my response:

Authority Magazine

Interviewer:

Let's begin with a basic definition so that we are all on the same page. How would you define an "Effective Communicator?" What are the characteristics of an effective communicator?

Me:

This makes me think of one of my favorite quotes:

"I've learned that people will forget what you said, people will forget what you did, but people will never forget how you made them feel." Maya Angelou

This perfectly sums up what I think an effective communicator is: someone who can make you feel.

Communication isn't about the words that you say. It's about the emotions, stories, and experiences behind your words.

To be an effective communicator, you need three traits: courage, passion, and authenticity.

Whether you're communicating in person, virtually, or even in writing, it takes courage to speak up and share your ideas. You're opening yourself up to criticism, offering your views that may not be widely accepted, and acknowledging when you make mistakes or don't know an answer. You need to have the courage to speak up in a crowd and do it with authority.

When you're speaking about something you're passionate about, that passion becomes contagious. Inject your energy and enthusiasm into what you're saying and those listening will mirror it back to you and be more engaged in what you're presenting. You become more trustworthy and more persuasive when you illustrate your passion because it helps you speak with conviction.

Finally, authenticity is paramount. Communicating in a way that is genuine and true to yourself will make you more effective because it builds trust and credibility. When you show your authentic self, you acknowledge your imperfections, highlight your uniqueness, and build connections with your audience that will make them want to see you succeed.

Embrace the traits of courage, passion, and authenticity as you set out to become a thought leader.

Remember, it's not about being the person who speaks the loudest. It's not about standing on a pedestal, preaching to the masses. It's about being in the crowd, sparking conversations that matter. It's about being the person who says what others are thinking but are too afraid to voice. It's not about getting people to buy what you're selling, but about getting them to buy into what you're saying.

Thought Leadership Self-Assessment Quiz

Instructions: Answer the following questions honestly. Choose the option that best represents your current approach or perspective. At the end of the quiz, tally your scores to see where you stand on your thought leadership journey.

How often do you share your professional insights or opinions publicly?

A Regularly, I publish articles, speak at events, or post on social media. (3 points)

B Occasionally, when I feel strongly about a topic. (2 points)

C Rarely or never. I usually keep my opinions to myself. (1 point)

When faced with a challenging situation in your field, you are more likely to:

A Develop innovative solutions and share them with others. (3 points)

B Stick to proven methods, but open to discussing new ideas. (2 points)

C Follow the lead of industry peers without much deviation. (1 point)

How do you react to new trends or changes in your industry?

A I analyze them, form my own opinions, and often lead discussions about them. (3 points)

B I keep informed and occasionally contribute to discussions. (2 points)

C I observe from the sidelines and follow the consensus. (1 point)

Your approach to professional networking is:

A Proactive. I seek to connect with diverse individuals and often initiate discussions. (3 points)

B Balanced. I network when necessary but don't often initiate. (2 points)

C Passive. I rarely network unless approached. (1 point)

When it comes to personal branding:

A I have a clear personal brand that reflects my unique perspective and expertise. (3 points)

B I have some sense of personal branding but haven't fully developed it. (2 points)

C I haven't really thought about personal branding. (1 point)

How do you view your role in your professional community?

A As a leader or an innovator who actively contributes to its growth. (3 points)

B As a participant who engages but doesn't necessarily lead. (2 points)

C As a spectator, mostly observing and following others. (1 point)

16-18 Points:

Emerging Thought Leader

You're actively engaged in shaping your industry, sharing your insights, and you have a strong foundation for becoming a thought leader. Focus on further developing your unique voice and expanding your influence.

10-15 Points:

Aspiring Thought Leader

You're on your way to becoming a thought leader. You engage with your industry but may need to take more initiative in sharing your ideas and establishing your personal brand.

6-9 Points:

Thought Leadership Novice

You're at the beginning of your thought leadership journey. Consider taking more active steps towards sharing your insights, building your network, and developing your personal brand.

Remember, thought leadership is a journey, not a destination. No matter where you score, there's always room to grow and influence your industry in your unique way.

Keep pushing boundaries, sharing your insights, and making an impact.

Business, Trust, and the Impact of Thought Leadership

Thought leadership is a topic commonly tied to branding. As we become thought leaders, we need to start thinking of ourselves as a brand and deciding whether or not our brand should be tied to a company.

Personal vs. Professional Brands

When it comes to personal and professional brands, we're basically comparing apples to… well, slightly bigger apples.

They're really not much different. For some (myself included) your personal brand is your professional brand. I am my company, my company is me. I can use my name and my brand name interchangeably because I own the company and am the only one intrinsically tied to it.

If you're an employee of a company, tying your personal brand to that company can be tricky. If you decide to leave or are let go, a piece of your identity is essentially gone.

Similarly, if you're an executive leader for a company with employees, stakeholders, and the like, your personal brand becomes a reflection of the professional brand. Your actions and decisions have the ability to impact everyone involved.

In all three scenarios, thought leadership is an option, we just have to approach it differently. When representing more than just yourself, ensure that all content you create and conversations you lead not only reflect positively on your brand but also align with the company's values.

If you'd like to explore the concept of branding further, you can find a free downloadable e-book titled *Build Your Brand: The 8 Components of a Brand That Sticks* in this book's content guide: www.favoritedaughtermedia.com/book.

Building Trust

Whether you're tied to a professional brand or simply representing yourself, your success will be fundamentally anchored in trust. The impact of that trust is what will differ.

Imagine the whole world losing trust in a company like Apple. Millions of people would be impacted—from simply having to trade in their Apple devices to losing their entire source of income. Now, if the entire world lost trust in me, the only person impacted would be... me. (Please don't, though. I've been told I'm a delight.)

Earning and keeping trust as a personal brand can be easier than it is for a big company for a few reasons. Your reach is smaller, giving you fewer people you need to keep happy. Your impact is smaller, reducing the stakes of a mishap. You're not being judged by the behaviors of others at the company. And, most importantly, you're just being yourself and you're visible.

It's easier to trust a person whose face you've seen, voice you've heard, and dog you've pet than a large company hiding behind a logo. If you know that by working with Favorite Daughter Media you're actually working with Sara, your mind shifts from seeing it as a company to seeing it as a person.

This is one of the reasons that realtors put their picture on park benches. Keller Williams Realty, Inc. feels like a big brand, but you've seen Brenda's face all over town. She almost feels like a friend. When you want to buy a house, you're calling Brenda.

As either a one-person show or a representative of a corporate giant, you want to lead with the personal, authentic side of you. People want to feel like they're interacting with a friend, not just a logo or a brand.

Trust and Authenticity

In chapter five, I talked about how telling authentic stories can build trust with an audience. When we tell stories from a professional platform, whether we're speaking as our own personal brand or representing a company, those stories still have the trust-building impact.

As a thought leader, we build trust based on two general factors: accuracy and authenticity.

I could get up in front of the United Nations and give a well-written, compelling speech explaining evidence that clouds are, in fact, made from cotton candy and if you open your mouth while skydiving you'll get a sweet little treat.

Would that speech enhance my credibility? Probably not, considering it's nonsense. As a thought leader, you need to be putting out content and information that, to the best of your knowledge, is accurate.

By continuously offering valuable information and thought-provoking insights, you build a strong relationship of trust with your audience and demonstrate your understanding of their needs and challenges.

The authenticity piece comes from combining that accurate information with personal stories and giving your audience the opportunity to get to know the person behind the brand.

The Impact of Trust on a Business

How much does trust impact the business world? It has become the new brand equity. Consumers today are savvy. They don't just buy products; they buy experiences, stories, and most significantly, they buy trust.

As a thought leader, when you become a beacon of authenticity, your business reaps the rewards. People are more likely to engage with a brand they feel they know, and what better way to know a brand than through its leader?

When a business leader shares authentic stories and reveals moments of vulnerability, they become a person rather than a company in the eyes of the consumer. And that's a good thing because consumer trust in businesses is pretty low.

Now, I know my whole mantra is to lead with stories, but sometimes we do need to throw in statistics to mix it up a little bit. This is one of those times.

According to PwC's 2023 Trust Survey[4], 84% of business executives thought that customers highly trust their company but only 27% of customers actually agreed. In the 2022 report[5], 33% of respondents reported they have paid premium prices for companies because they trust them and 91% say they would buy from a company that gained their trust.

The 2021 Edelman Trust Barometer Special Report[6] surveyed 14,000 people across 14 countries. Here are some of the findings:

88% said that trust was important, or even critical, when deciding which brands to buy from.

Consumers are seven times more likely to buy from brands they trust.

68% of respondents say that trusting a brand is more important now than in the past, with trust being more significant among younger generations than older ones.

63% say they'd rather support a brand that they trust has a mission to better the world.

40% have stopped supporting brands they loved because they lost trust in the company, increasing to 50% among high income respondents.

Consumers are 61% more likely to become advocates for brands they fully trust.

Other Impacts of Thought Leadership

While building trust is vital for success, it's not the only way thought leadership can impact a business.

Magnifying Your Reach

Consistently putting out valuable content will help your business reach more people. Thought leadership acts as a megaphone for your business. As you share your insights on platforms, at conferences, and in publications, you're echoing your thoughts, and you're amplifying your brand's presence.

Opportunities for Partnerships

Collaborations and partnerships often arise when peers recognize and respect your authority in the field. So, by being a thought leader, you're inadvertently weaving a web of opportunities for your business.

Enhancing Brand Visibility and Recognition

Thought leadership helps with increasing the visibility of your brand. By sharing your insights on various platforms like industry publications, social media, and speaking engagements, you can reach a wider audience. This increased exposure contributes to brand recognition and recall.

Differentiating Your Brand

Thought leadership allows you to differentiate your brand from competitors. In a market where many businesses may offer similar products or services, your unique insights and perspectives set you apart, showcasing your brand's unique value proposition.

Attracting Top Talent

Companies known for their thought leadership are often seen as desirable places to work. This helps in attracting top talent who are eager to work for a company that's a leader in its field.

Influencing Industry Trends and Conversations

Thought leaders have the power to influence trends and conversations within their industry. This can put your brand at the forefront of new movements and innovations, giving you a competitive edge.

What to Remember

Thought Leadership isn't Just About Making Noise, But Sparking Change: While influencers focus on what's on the surface, thought leaders dive deeper, challenge the status quo, and invite others to explore new ideas with them.

It's a Mix of Expertise and Humanity: Yes, being a thought leader means you have expertise in a subject. But it's not just about what you know—it's about how you relate. Sharing your journey, the ups and downs, is what breathes life into your expertise and makes people want to listen.

Leading Versus Selling: Thought leaders ignite conversations and inspire actions based on ideas they believe in, not products they want to sell. They make you pause, think, and see the world a bit differently.

What to Do Now

Think about a few people who you truly trust.

What made you trust them? Can you remember a trait, story, or moment that made you feel like you could rely on them? Write about what they did (or didn't do) to make you trust them and how you can apply that to help build trust for you within others.

Journal

Journal

Journal

Journal

"Trust is built and maintained by many small actions over time."

Lolly Daskal

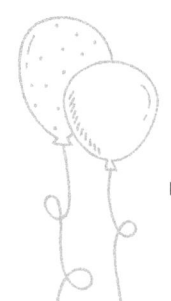
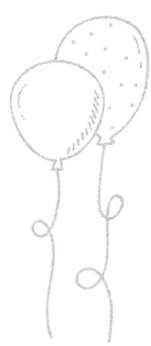

Chapter 9

The Know, Like, Trust Process

Trust is key, but how exactly can we build it through storytelling? The cornerstone of personal branding, thought leadership, and sales is a concept called Know, Like, Trust. This is a journey you guide your audience through to transform them from casual listeners to dedicated followers.

Make Them Know You

The first time you meet a person at a party, what do you do? You introduce yourself. Or, if you're like me, you hope the one friend you've been following around who dragged you to the party introduces you to them because you're shy and have social anxiety.

Regardless, all social interactions start with an introduction. The Know phase is your introduction. It's you putting your personal brand on display for the world to see.

In your Know phase, you start creating content—blogs, podcasts, social media posts. Whatever your preferred avenue. But you do it in a way that centers on who you are and begins to tell your story.

The first thing I did when I launched Favorite Daughter Media was publish a blog (or, as it's branded on my website, a diary entry) titled "Why Am I Doing This?"

Here it is:

Dear Diary,

I did it. I took the plunge. I sent the text that said, "I think I'm ready to go independent."

Now, did I expect leaving my current career to have a little more fanfare than a late-night, not-at-all-thought-out text message to the CEO of my company? Yeah, a little bit. But here we are.

So, why did I send the text? I've been asking myself that for a few weeks now. I've had regrets, anxiety attacks, deep feelings of relief, and overwhelming feelings of self doubt. And yet, I still think it was the right thing to do.

I've spent the past three years working in the financial planning world. I have learned more about retirement accounts than I ever thought I'd know, made a bigger impact on the industry than I've yet grasped, and found a passion for personal finance at 25 that 20-year-old me never saw coming.

But despite all I've learned—even in becoming an Accredited Financial Counselor—one of the biggest realizations I've had is that I am not a financial professional.

Don't get me wrong, I can teach you about paying yourself first, hacking your HSA, and leaving a financial legacy until I'm blue in the face and you kindly remind me that you never asked, but that doesn't make me a financial professional. It makes me a money nerd, sure. But not a financial professional.

In an industry full of khaki pants and tucked-in, neutral-toned polo shirts for casual Friday, I live my life with far more color. I collect tattoos as souvenirs because this body took me on such wonderful adventures, it feels right to etch them on my skin. I dye my hair pink sometimes because I get tired of looking at plain blonde, but learned not to dye it blue because it will quickly fade to a sickly green and refuse to wash out. I find it hard not to cuss in inappropriate moments and would rather wear jeans and sundresses than pantsuits and pinstripes.

I probably should've figured this part out long ago. It would've saved my coworkers a lot of frustration as they realized for the 84th time that no, I did not log that email into Salesforce because no, I do not know what that means.

My brain doesn't work in Salesforce. I'd be happy to design a presentation that explains how my brain does work, but it would be several very pretty slides that all say, "I don't know." I have a creator's brain, and does any creator really know what that means?

So, after realizing far too late that my inability to follow dishearteningly dull orders of operation was causing my coworkers additional stress, I decided to take myself out of the equation (see, finance puns are fun). Thankfully, I had options.

In 2021, my CEO, a gem of a coworker, and I joined forces to launch a consultancy that was meant to allow the CEO to pass on his years of wisdom as a business owner and advisor to others in similar positions. I was to play a small role helping those clients improve their marketing as well.

Turns out, far more advisors wanted to work with me than him. Not because he isn't great (I mean, I didn't realize so many financial designations existed), but because it is much easier to admit that you need help with a task that is not your speciality than one that is. At least, that's my perspective. I could be wrong.

I started working with other firms, either coaching their teams or becoming their marketing person, and was able to make an impact on not only my company but others as well. So, when I decided it was time to go independent, I was able to do it while bringing my job with me.

By some miracle, I had built enough trust and proven my skills so that the company that employed me offered me a contract to become my client. I worked out an agreement that any financial entity that wished to work with me could do so under the brand of the consulting firm that I helped to grow.

Could anything be more perfect? I could step away from the administrative tasks that haunted me and focus on the marketing and creation that brought me so much joy.

But still, it was all financial. I love finance. I made that clear. But I still felt like I could be doing more with my messy creator brain if I wasn't tied to such a buttoned-up and regulated industry. I wanted to build my own brand that could work on projects that let me use more puns and silly words and laugh at myself and laugh with others.

I launched Favorite Daughter as my creative outlet because after years of using just a smidgen of my creativity to help financial brands thrive, I wanted to see what I could do if I was set loose and allowed to truly be myself. So, it's time to find some clients who will believe in me as much as my (former) CEO does. If you want to be that client, reach out. I can't wait to see what we can create together.

SHARE ON SOCIALS

I was very intentional in how I wrote this blog. I talked about who I was, what I was passionate about, and why I was starting this new chapter of my career. I let people get to know me exactly as I am.

You need to do that, too. In this phase, choose stories that help people know you:

Your origin story.

How did you get to where you are? What hurdles did you have to overcome? Show yourself as relatable and approachable.

Your milestone stories.

What significant goals have you reached recently? Have you accomplished something meaningful? Celebrate your wins in public so people know what it is that you do and thank those who helped you along the way.

Your insights.

Share stories that highlight your expertise. What problem did you recently solve for a client? How did you solve it? What discovery did you make that simplified a process? Don't tell someone you're an expert, show them that you are.

Make Them Like You

Once people know you, you need them to connect with you on a deeper, emotional level. You need them to like you. This is when you start to show off your personality.

Let's go back to that party. Now that you've been introduced, you can start to relax, be yourself, and interact with the other partygoers.

Are you the life of the party, standing in the middle of the crowd telling that great story you have about that thing you did? Are you the free spirit, dancing to the music while others watch and cheer?

Start to let your personality show so people can know the real you, not just your name and logo. People are more likely to engage with someone they like.

One of my first attempts at this was in a diary entry called "Can You Keep a Secret?," in which I showed vulnerability and authenticity.

Can you keep a secret?

Dear Diary,

I have a secret I've been hesitant to share. But in the spirit of being fully authentic, I want to let you in on it:

drum roll please

I don't love guesting on podcasts.

I know, it's pretty scandalous.

So why would I launch a company based solely on podcast guesting? Because I know it works!

When I say I don't love it, I only mean that I don't love to do it myself. I am naturally introverted. I do not like public speaking. I have major imposter syndrome and am certainly my worse critic.

Podcast hosts have been kind enough to invite me on their shows and I am honored to accept. Still, part of me worries that while I know the science behind guesting and have helped others to do it greatly, I lack the confidence in myself to really make the impact that I want to make.

I have spent my career behind the scenes—producing, editing, booking, coaching, writing, designing—and taking the leap onto the mic is so far out of my comfort zone. I am new at this. And like everything else, it takes practice.

As episodes and interviews come out, I ask you this: give me grace. I am still honing my own message and building my confidence in front of an audience. My comfort zone is in what I hope to do for my clients—the creation and strategy—but I must step out of it if I want to grow as a business owner and as a person.

Thank you for keeping my secret. I'm slowly becoming a better me.

SHARE ON SOCIALS

The stories you tell while in the Like phase should be transparent and honest. Tell these kinds of stories:

Tales of the underdog.

People love to root for an underdog. If you've faced adversity and come out stronger, share that journey.

A day in the life.

What's your daily routine like? What challenges do you face every day? How do you overcome them? Let people into your world so they can see the real you.

What's your why?

Why do you do what you do? Are you trying to make an impact on society? Provide for a family? Make your parents proud? Sharing your why helps others become invested in your success and want to see you through it.

Make Them Trust You

The final stage is, arguably, the most important. Trust is the VIP pass to the party. The golden ticket. When someone trusts you, it means they believe in your expertise, your integrity, and your recommendations. This is when they transform from followers to advocates. This is when they decide to invest in you.

In this part of my own journey, I focused on diary entries that were more informative than narrative. I shared insights, best practices, and examples of interviews or talks I had done.

You still want to tell a story, but you want it to highlight what you know. Tell these stories:

Case studies and testimonials.

What real world examples can you share of how you added value for someone else?

Transparent recounts.

Ever made a mistake? Faced a setback? Sharing these stories and how you learned from them can enhance your credibility.

Continuous learning.

Share your journey of growth and learning. Did you attend a seminar? Read a thought provoking book? Hear a podcast that changed your perspective? Talk about it.

While I won't include a specific entry, I have diary entries of conference recaps, things I learned from podcast hosts who interviewed me, and even my top five books I read during the year. I want people to trust that I am constantly looking to learn so that I am constantly adding to what I can teach.

What to Remember

Let People Know You: Introduce yourself by showcasing your personal brand, sharing your origin story, milestones, and insights to establish your identity and expertise. Lay your cards on the table and let them see you, not your brand.

Make People Like You: Reveal your personality and values through authentic, transparent stories. Start building emotional connections by sharing your underdog tales, daily routines, and personal motivations, making you relatable and likable.

Help People Trust You: Demonstrate your expertise and integrity by sharing case studies, learning experiences, and transparent recounts of challenges. Prove your knowledge and commitment to growth, solidifying trust with your audience.

What to Do Now

Reflect on your journey through the Know, Like, Trust process. Describe how you introduced yourself or personal brand, developed emotional connections, and established trust. What stories and experiences did you share at each stage of this process? If you haven't started, which stories could you tell at each stage?

Journal

Journal

Journal

"The top experts in the world are ardent students. The day you stop learning, you're definitely not an expert."

Brendon Burchard

Chapter 10

What Are You Talking About?

We all know a lot about a lot of things, but how do we know we're an expert in them?

First, let's talk about what an expert is, because it means so many things to so many people.

Emily Crookston of The Pocket PhD[7] talked to several experts and came to these conclusions:

- *Few experts wholeheartedly embrace the "expert" label or naturally describe themselves as such.*

- *Expertise is best described as a process, not an end-result.*

- *Experts ask thought-provoking questions and give reflective answers.*

- *Every expert has a self-awareness practice, even if they wouldn't call it such.*

- *"Boredom" is not in the expert's vocabulary.*

Some people follow the 10,000 hour rule, an idea introduced by Malcolm Gladwell that says you need to practice something for 10,000 hours before you're an expert. By definition, an expert is somebody who has a broad and deep understanding and competence in terms of knowledge, skill, and experience. In the court of law, an expert witness can be anyone with knowledge or experience beyond that of a layperson.

Crookston gave two suggestions of what stand at the core of expertise:

- *Being able to look at something you've done a hundred or a thousand times before with a beginner's mind.*

- *Being able to find something interesting, new, and different in each moment.*

I love this idea of expertise. It suggests that expertise lies within curiosity —that what we know is not nearly as important as our desire to know more.

To be a thought leader, you need to be an expert.

Let's move forward with the assumption that an expert is someone who not only knows a lot about a topic, but is continiously learning more. An expert is someone who is curious.

To be endlessly curious is to recognize that no matter how much you know, there is always more to learn. It's to understand that with every question answered, several new questions will emerge.

I want you to lean into your curiosity with the reckless abandon of a small child holding a magnifying glass: run through the backyard of your industry, look under rocks in search of microscopic worlds, peek around corners that lead to the unknown, dive deeper into the rabbit hole without worrying about getting mud on your new shirt.

We can learn a lot about curiosity from kids, but we can also learn a lot about passion.

When we were kids, we (or at least me) were always being told to use our inside voices. Sometimes we were told this when we weren't even indoors. We were always told we needed to speak more quietly, even if we were so excited we felt like we would burst if we didn't yell it for the world to hear.

That level of passion and excitement can be rare as we reach adulthood and feel obligated to use our inside voices.

I encourage you to use your outside voice. Tell your stories loudly so they can be heard from the back of the room. Have your "eureka!" moments at full volume. Embrace your expertise by exploring what you've yet to discover, and sing out your findings as loudly as you want to.

Stay Curious

Being an expert doesn't mean you've reached the pinnacle of understanding; it means you're committed to the climb, always seeking, always questioning. You're sharing the journey, the missteps, the detours, and the views from the top with anyone willing to walk the path with you.

Here are some ways to stay curious:

Embrace being a newbie
As kids, we learned or tried something new every day. As adults, it's more rare. But there's something magical about looking at a topic with fresh eyes. It's like being a kid in a candy store. Everything's fascinating and colorful and exciting. Stay curious by remembering there's always something to be learned if you're willing to try something new.

Mix things up
Don't just stick to your lane. Cross over to other fields, listen to different voices, and let those unique perspectives challenge and enrich your understanding.

Ask questions
Then ask some more. Be that person who's always wondering why, how, or what if. Not only does it keep your brain engaged, but it might also lead you down paths you never considered exploring.

Teach and share
There's nothing like teaching to make you realize how much you don't know. Sharing your knowledge with others not only helps solidify what you do know but also opens up avenues for learning you might not have encountered otherwise.

Learn to love the unknown

Get comfortable with not having all the answers. It's not a sign of weakness; it's an open invitation to learn more. Every "I don't know" is just the start of a new adventure.

What Do You Want to Talk About?

Thought leadership isn't just about being an authority or an expert, but sharing your ideas in ways that sparks curiosity in others. And we do that through stories.

When you're figuring out what you want to talk about—the topic that makes you use your outside voice—think about it from the perspective of the little kid with the magnifying glass.

What do you get excited to talk about? What are you constantly looking for more information on? What podcasts do you fall asleep listening to?

When we shift our focus from "I am an expert in" to "I am passionate about," we may realize that what we want to share our thoughts on is not what we originally thought.

On a professional level, I know a lot about personal finance. I know a lot about podcast production. I know marketing strategies that work and ones that don't. But that doesn't excite me.

This does.

I get excited when I listen to someone tell a good story. I get lost in audiobooks that have great narrative arcs. I wrote this book not because I think I know everything about storytelling and thought leadership, but because I wanted to know more. I know so much more as I finish writing this book than I did when I started. The research that I've done and the stories that I've read have me wanting others to read this book just so I have someone to talk about it with.

In the year since I began writing, I've rewritten this book at least four times because I kept learning more that I wanted to share. I've changed the title, changed the format, changed the entire topic and focus because I was willing to stay curious during the process and accept that I don't know everything.

If we go back to the beginning of this book, I told you that I believe we are all anthologies. Think of your life or your professional journey as an epic saga of curiosity and expertise.

Each chapter is filled with quests for knowledge, battles with challenges, and moments of revelation. Now, think about sharing these stories— not just what happened but why and how and what you may have done differently if the book of your life allowed for rewrites.

This is where thought leadership and storytelling intertwine, transforming individual experiences into universal lessons.

Your stories of curiosity—the questions that keep you up at night, the mysteries you're dying to unravel—become more than personal anecdotes. They're invitations to your audience to question, to challenge, and to be curious alongside you. These stories don't just tell; they engage, inspire, and provoke thought, laying the groundwork for a community of learners and thinkers.

What you need to do now is decide exactly what you want to be talking about. Think about the topics that excite you most—the ones that have filled your head and heart with endless amounts of stories—and stake your claim in that arena.

Write those stories in your blog. Post bite-sized pearls of wisdom on social media. Find podcasts that cover that topic and become a listener and a guest. Research events where your topic would hold relevance and submit to be a speaker.

You know what you want to talk about. It's time to start talking.

What to Remember

Expertise is a Journey of Curiosity: True expertise is framed not as a destination reached but as a continuous journey fueled by endless curiosity. Constantly seek new knowledge and perspectives, push the boundaries of what you understand, and embrace a beginner's mindset, no matter how seasoned you might become.

Passion is the Driving Force: Passion is what propels us to dive deeper, explore further, and share louder. Channel the unbridled enthusiasm of your inner child, allowing your outside voice to resonate with others and ignite their curiosity and excitement.

Storytelling is a Tool for Engagement: Sharing our journey of curiosity and expertise through stories transforms abstract concepts into relatable experiences. It's through storytelling that thought leaders can provoke thought, inspire action, and instill a sense of shared adventure in discovery.

What to Do Now

What are the topics that make you need to use your outside voice? List them out and write about why they excite you, the specific ideas that come to mind, and the stories that you'd share with an audience.

Journal

Journal

Journal

Journal

"There are only two types of speakers in the world. The nervous and the liars."

Mark Twain

Chapter 11

The Avenues to Thought Leadership

Becoming a thought leader isn't a one-size-fits-all journey. We choose the avenue that aligns with our passions, talents, and abilities.

There are several avenues you can use, each with its own set of advantages and challenges. For a well-rounded personal branding and thought leadership plan, you may want to use several or all of them.

Podcasting

Podcasting is my favorite form of media and is a powerful avenue towards thought leadership.

Podcasting allows you to share your expertise in a conversational and accessible manner. With a podcast, you can dive deep into topics, create a content library, and attract a dedicated audience. It's a way to share your knowledge, personality, and viewpoints on a regular basis, contributing to the Know, Like, Trust cycle.

Podcasting is built on community and authentic connections. To be a great podcast guest or host, you need to be willing to give yourself to the listener through the stories that you tell.

Your aim for each episode should be to deliver as much value as you're able.

Advantages

Personal connections: You have the ability to convey a lot of personality and emotion through just your voice, allowing listeners to form strong connections with you and feel like they're part of the conversation.

Flexibility: Podcasts can be listened to anywhere while doing nearly anything.

Niche appeal: Podcasts target very specific audiences with very specific interests, making them great for specialized subjects.

Challenges

Technical barriers: Setting up a podcast requires a good amount of technical prowess, including recording, editing, and publishing. You'll need to either learn to do it or have the budget to pay a professional.

Consistency: Being consistent with recording and releasing episodes can be demanding if you have a busy schedule—especially if you're handling all of it on your own.

Slow growth: Building a podcast audience and community takes time and requires strategic marketing efforts.

Podcasting Best Practices

Be consistent: Choose a schedule for releasing episodes and stick to it.

Collaborate: Interviewing experts and thought leaders can expand your network and grow your audience. Even better, collaborating with other podcasters by trading guest appearances and promoting each others' shows is one of the fastest ways to grow your listenership.

Engage: Use social media to promote your episodes, ask for listener questions, and be responsive to messages and feedback.

Public speaking is a common avenue for thought leadership. This could mean speaking at events for other organizations, like conferences, summits, and industry events, or creating your own stages by hosting seminars, webinars, and workshops.

Public speaking is very polarizing. You either love it or hate it. And it takes more than confidence and delivery.

There are courses all over the internet that can teach you cadence and how to stand with better posture and what you're supposed to do with your hands. (Please, let me know if you learn that last one. I am at a loss.)

But there is something that every speaker needs that can't be taught in a course: the willingness to be vulnerable. Use your stories on stage and captivate every person in the room. You'll stand out from other speakers and be remembered by your listeners.

Advantages

Instant feedback: Unlike other formats, public speaking allows immediate interaction with your audience, which is very rewarding.

High impact: A successful speech quickly elevates your status within your industry.

Networking: Speaking engagements are often at events where there's a high potential for meeting people to add to your network.

Challenges

Stage fright: Public speaking isn't for everyone; it requires a comfort level with being the center of attention.

Preparation: A good talk requires substantial prep work, including research, slide creation, and rehearsal.

Limited reach: Unlike digital formats, the impact of a live speech is confined to the time and place of the event, although this can be mitigated by recording it.

Public Speaking Best Practices

Quality over quantity: Instead of speaking at every opportunity, choose platforms that best align with your expertise and target audience.

Engage and interact: Use Q&A sessions, interactive polls, and live demonstrations to make your talk more engaging.

Follow-up: Connect with attendees afterward via social media and email. Offer takeaway materials such as slides, checklists, and whitepapers as lead magnets.

Publishing

Writing a book on a topic gives you nearly instant authority as a thought leader. Choose a topic you are passionate about and write about it in a way that expresses expertise, introduces unique points of view, and incorporates your experience and stories.

Publishing adds gravitas to your personal brand. A well-researched paper or a comprehensive book serves as a cornerstone for your expertise, providing tangible proof of your in-depth knowledge.

Publishing doesn't have to mean a hardcover novel sold at Barnes and Noble. You can write a short e-book or white paper, save it as a PDF, and publish it on your own website as a free download or sell it through a platform like Etsy or Shopify.

Advantages

Credibility: Having a published paper or book is a strong credential that lends academic or professional credibility.

Long Shelf Life: Published works often continue to be cited and read over many years, providing long-term benefits.

Deep Exploration: The format allows for a deep dive into complex subjects, which showcases your depth of knowledge.

Challenges

Time-Consuming: The research, writing, and editing process is time-intensive.

Barrier to Entry: High-quality journals and publishers have stringent requirements and peer-review processes. Self-publishing, however, is a viable option for any aspiring author.

Limited Audience: Academic and specialized publications may not reach a broad audience, especially if they're behind paywalls.

Publishing Best Practices

Choose Your Platform: Whether it's academic journals, industry magazines, or self-publishing, pick the platform that reaches your target audience best.

Promote: Simply publishing isn't enough. Use your existing platforms like social media, a blog, or a newsletter to promote your work.

Collaborate: Co-authoring expands your reach and brings additional perspectives, making your content richer, with less effort.

Content Creation

Thought leadership can come in the form of valuable and insightful online content. Blog posts, videos, and articles about a certain topic that are unique, compelling, and informative can position you as an industry expert.

Even micro-content, like what we see on social media, helps you engage with the public and build an audience.

Advantages

Broad reach: Content in the form of blogs, vlogs, and social media posts are able to reach a global audience.

Creativity: The format allows for a lot of creative freedom; you can mix and match media types and topics to keep things interesting.

SEO benefits: Regularly updated, valuable content helps improve your search engine rankings.

Challenges

Content overload: The internet is flooded with content, making it difficult to stand out.

Quality control: Consistently producing high-quality content requires a solid strategy and a good understanding of your audience's needs.

Commitment: Content creation is a long-term commitment that requires regular updates to keep the audience engaged.

Content Creation Best Practices

Consistency: Whether it's a weekly blog post or a daily social media update, be consistent.

Quality over quantity: Make sure your content adds value; otherwise, it becomes noise.

Engage: Respond to comments, ask for feedback, and encourage audience interaction to build community.

Additional Ideas

YouTube and Video Content

Creating video content on platforms like YouTube allows you to visually engage with your audience. This can range from educational content to interviews and commentary on industry trends.

Online Courses and Workshops

Creating and teaching online courses and conducting workshops is a direct way to share your expertise and educate others, thereby building your reputation as a knowledgeable leader in your field.

Networking Events and Panel Discussions

Participating in networking events and panel discussions can elevate your status as a thought leader, especially when you share unique insights and engage in meaningful discussions.

Collaborations and Guest Contributions

Collaborating with other experts or contributing as a guest writer or speaker on various platforms helps expand your reach and add credibility to your thought leadership.

Newsletters and Email Marketing

Regular newsletters allow you to stay in touch with your audience, sharing insights, updates, and valuable content directly.

Community Engagement and Forums

Actively participating in relevant online communities and forums (like Reddit, Quora, or industry-specific platforms) can build your reputation as a helpful and knowledgeable leader.

Which avenue feels right to you? Jot down your thoughts about how you could leverage these different media, and some ideas for getting started.

Journal

Journal

Journal

Journal

> "It takes courage to grow up and
> become who you really are."
>
> E. E. Cummings

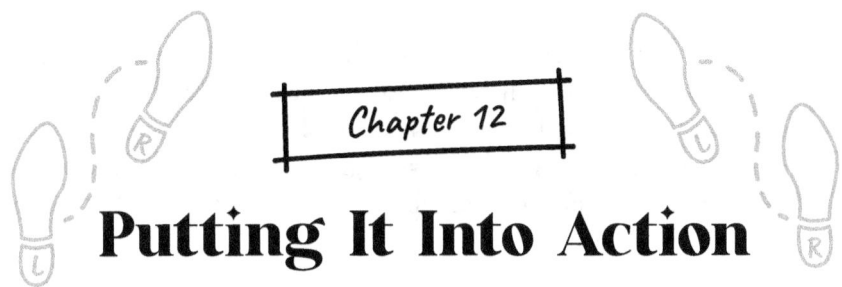

Chapter 12

Putting It Into Action

There's a common saying that "facts tell, stories sell." I believe this is is true, but we're not just trying to sell something here. We're aiming to grab attention, spark curiosity, and maybe, just maybe, light up that bulb of inspiration in someone's mind.

So, what's the secret to balancing our knowledge with the kind of storytelling that keeps people engaged?

Every time you're talking to a client, brainstorming with your team, or standing in the spotlight at a workshop, you're not just talking; you're leading a dance. A dance where your stories set the rhythm and your expertise picks up the beat. The stories are what lead and the facts are what follow.

Stories humanize us. They peel back the layers, showing off the wins, the whoopsies, and those little moments of magic that make us, well, us. They're like open invitations, saying, "Hey, come on in. Let's go on this ride together."

Every story you share should have a purpose. Lead your audience down a path where every twist and turn reveals a bit more about who you are and the 'whys' behind your drive.

While your stories are out there making connections, your expertise is cementing your credibility. It's the backbone that assures your audience you're not just a great storyteller, but you've got the chops to back it up. Your achievements and insights are gold, but without a story they may as well just be another trophy on the shelf.

To intertwine stories and expertise, start by identifying the pivotal moments in your journey that led to where you are. Was there a eureka moment that pushed you into your field? Was there a particular challenge that, once overcome, set you on your path?

When pitching to a client or presenting a talk, start with a story. If a dietitian begins by sharing her own battles with food and body image before diving into the science of nutrition, she captures attention and creates connections because we've all struggled with self confidence in our lives. She set the stage and now her expertise can shine, grounded in a story that hits close to home.

While knowing your story and expertise is crucial, understanding your audience is the final piece of the puzzle. Consider their needs, their expectations, and their current understanding of your topic.

Every time you dive into an expert topic, think of a related story that enhances your message. Talking about a complex concept? Share a client success story. Breaking down a business strategy? Tell them about the time it turned the tide for you.

Remember to keep your stories tight—beginning, middle, end—then swing straight into the solid advice. It's like putting together a conference session; you outline what's in it, who's behind it, and what attendees will walk away with.

I like to do this by actually putting my stories into a conference session format. If you've ever spoken at, applied to speak at, or even attended a conference, you know what this is.

Here's the format

> **Title:** What Your Story Is Called
>
> **Subtitle:** The Point of Your Story
>
> **Description:** What your story is about, who should listen to it, and what they'll learn.
>
> **Key Takeaways:** Three to five nuggets of wisdom that can be derived from your story.

It's the way each session is outlined on the agenda. The purpose of this outline is to let attendees know what the session is about, who is presenting it, and what they will learn from attending.

How do you make your story worth attending?

Being a thought leader demands a duality: the empathy of a storyteller and the intellect of an expert. The magic is in combining them seamlessly. As you grow professionally, let your stories and expertise feed off each other, enriching your journey and sharing greater insights with your audience.

So, don't hesitate. Dive into your memories, draw from your lessons, and lead with authenticity. Use the following pages to start outlining your own stories.

Here's a braindump space

Story 1

Title: _____

Subtitle: _____

Description: _____
_____
_____
_____

Key Takeaways:

1. _____

2. _____

3. _____

4. _____

5. _____

Story 2

Title: _____

Subtitle: _____

Description: _____
_____
_____

Key Takeaways:

1. _____

2. _____

3. _____

4. _____

5. _____

Story 3

Title: _____

Subtitle: _____

Description: _____

_____

_____

Key Takeaways:

1. _____

2. _____

3. _____

4. _____

5. _____

Story 4

Title: _____

Subtitle: _____

Description: _____

_____

_____

Key Takeaways:

1. _____

2. _____

3. _____

4. _____

5. _____

Congratulations, you've reached the final chapter of a book that I hope has been as enlightening for you to read as it has been fulfilling for me to write.

This is not the end, just the point where we need to decide what comes next.

Together, we've established that everyone has a unique and valuable story, and simply needs to find the best ways and places for telling it.

We defined thought leadership and how we can join the global conversation. We established what it means to be an expert, an influencer, and a leader in today's society. And we learned how and why we must use our outside voices.

Now for the real fun. Here are some steps to get you started:

1. Finish your story.

If you followed the writing prompts and completed the journal entries in the book, you should have a good idea of what your story is. I hope you have notes and scribbles and ideas that will keep you thinking long after you close this book.

Keep writing. Keep finding those stories hidden in your memory and extracting the value that they hold.

2. Choose your platform.

Which avenue of thought leadership would you like to take? Are you a talker or a writer? A podcaster or a film maker?

Do more research on the avenues available and find the ones that align with you. If you want to brainstorm ideas and talk about how each platform could work for you, book time in my calendar by visiting this book's content guide at www.favoritedaughtermedia.com/book.

3. Start small, but think big.

You don't have to launch a full-fledged book or podcast series right away. Begin where you are, with what you have. That might mean a thoughtful post on LinkedIn, a quick video on Instagram, or a mini-series on YouTube.

Practice using these platforms and sharing your story. As you get more comfortable, begin planning for how you can spread your message further and be heard by more people.

4. Continue to learn and grow.

Continuous learning is so important. Whether you're learning more about the topic you talk about, the platform you want to use, or just what's going on with the world, keep going.

Learn, read, and listen to other thought leaders who inspire you. The resource page for this book has some of my favorite content that has inspired me. Take a look if you need a place to start.

You're at the starting line of an incredible journey so I encourage you to take that first step. Tell your story. Share your expertise. Be your authentic self. Because the world doesn't just need more "experts"—it needs thought leaders who inspire, guide, and have a meaningful impact.

Start using your outside voice because the world is waiting to hear your story.

5. Reach out to me.

If you found this book helpful and would like to work with me on developing your story, I offer one-on-one coaching sessions on all of the topics covered.

Send me an email at sara@favoritedaughtermedia.com or reach out on my website, www.favoritedaughtermedia.com.

If this book helped you discover your own story, please send it to me. I would be honored to read it.

Acknowledgements

Thank you to everyone who helped this book get opened.

Larry Roberts

Jasmine Designs

Vince Warnock

Kim Thompson-Pinder

Danielle Lewis

Eric Brotman

Amanda Paolicelli

Alexandra Segel

Shannon Russell

Barbara McCoy

Sources

[1]Cleveland Clinic. (2022, April 4). What's imposter syndrome and how to overcome it

[2]Stevens, G. J., Silbert, L. J., & Hasson, U. (2010). Speaker–listener neural coupling underlies successful communication. Proceedings of the National Academy of Sciences, 107(32).

[3]Zak, P. J. (2014, November 5). Why Your Brain Loves Good Storytelling. Harvard Business Review.

[4]PricewaterhouseCoopers. 2023 Trust Survey: 9 Key Findings and Lessons for Business Executives

[5]PricewaterhouseCoopers. Trust: The New Currency for Business. https://www.pwc.com/us/en/services/consulting/library/consumer-intelligence-series/trust-new-business-currency.html

[6]Edelman. (2021, January 13). 2021 Edelman Trust Baramoter. https://www.edelman.com/trust/2021-trust-barometer

[7]Crookston, E. (2021, November 17). What Does it Mean to Be an Expert? The Pocket PhD. https://www.thepocketphd.com/2021/11/17/what-does-it-mean-to-be-an-expert/

.

About the Author

Sara Lohse is a storyteller, marketer, and brand architect with a knack for turning narratives into connections. Through Favorite Daughter Media, Sara uses her passion and talent to help mission-driven brands amplify their impact, proving that authentic storytelling and strategic marketing go hand in hand.

Sara's work and expertise, featured on conference stages including FinCon, PodFest Multimedia Expo, and Speakonomics and in publications such as Authority Magazine, showcase her as a gifted creator fueled by passion and caffeine, dedicated to making a difference through powerful storytelling and marketing.

www.ingramcontent.com/pod-product-compliance
Lightning Source LLC
Chambersburg PA
CBHW070656130626
46553CB00005B/1729